RISK
in Action

RISK

in Action

A Leader's Guide to
Act with Clarity

Jim Massey

Eastward

Chevy Chase, MD

First edition: October 11, 2025

Cover and book design by Sheila Parr

Hardcover ISBN: 979-8-9876976-3-4
Paperback ISBN: 979-8-9876976-4-1
Ebook ISBN: 979-8-9876976-5-8

Published by Eastward
www.jimmassey.co

Dedication

*This is for those willing to face what is uncertain, frame
it with meaning, and move forward with clarity.*

Trust yourself.

Be courageously fearFULL.

Act with clarity.

Be and do good.

Only those who will risk going too far can possibly find out how far one can go.

— **T. S. Eliot**

RISK
in Action

Contents

Acknowledgments

After writing *Trust in Action* and working alongside so many leaders, I began to see more clearly that trust, while essential, was not enough. Trust alone could not ensure action would be taken, especially when those I worked with found themselves at the edge of what was known, staring into the gap between where we were and where we needed to be. In time, I realized it was not only their struggle I was witnessing. I was stopping myself too. I knew what it felt like to stand at that edge and pretend that stillness was enough, to convince myself that waiting would somehow close the gap, rather than admit the harder truth that I could not remain as I was.

In that honesty, I realized something deeper: We have been looking at risk the wrong way. With change now our constant companion, our relationship with risk has to shift—so that all of us can move forward into what comes next. And this forced me once again to figuratively put pen to paper, examine my own risk aversion to technology and artificial intelligence, and move forward with a risk model I have relied on for years to lead teams into the uncharted and unknown with courage.

From cover to cover, this book is not mine alone.

To my sons, Sawyer and Lawson, you show me how important it is to adapt and keep moving. You bring a fresh perspective to old ways of thinking, and most importantly, you remind me that the risks worth taking are always the ones bound to love.

My family, friends, and framily (friends who are family) are my grounding force. You remind me that focus is not a narrowing of life but a widening of devotion, and that clarity is not about having every answer, but about choosing to move forward together, again and again.

The leaders I have walked beside have shown me that courage is never abstract. It unmasks itself inside clarity, in the moments when forward motion is hardest. You have reminded me that risk is always most real when it is shared.

Scott, my publishing coach once again, guided me with the steady hand of experience and the sharpness of a trusted friend. He reminded me that putting risk in action is a discipline, and that every page is a chance to choose it.

Ariella, as chief of staff for Eastward, helped me learn the AI way of writing. She carried ideas forward and always created space for imagination. She has been a voice of possibility in every step.

Sheila gave these models shape and color, turning thought into design and design into invitation. From the book cover to page layout to the diagrams within, her work brings meaning to my words and breathes life into ideas that might otherwise remain abstract.

Sarah, my copy editor, made these pages sing. Her incredible eye for detail and nuanced ear for writing have shepherded this book through the final mile, making it not just good, but great.

And to those of you who are reading, thank you. Every idea here only matters if it becomes part of your practice. My invitation is simple: Face risk with honesty, frame it with meaning, and keep moving forward. The rest of the journey is yours.

Introduction

Welcome *to the* Gap

"For fuck's sake, Massey, you've outgrown your companies. Don't take another corporate job."

Angela Barfield didn't sugarcoat anything. This thirty-five-year executive coaching veteran was 100 pounds soaking wet, but she was a force of nature who had just delivered some of the most important career advice I'd ever received. It was 2020, and I was paying her to help me figure out what the hell I was supposed to do next.

She was right, and I knew it. I just didn't want to say it. Knowing something and acting on it are two completely different things.

So I did what I'd always done. I avoided the big, risky, unknown space of entrepreneurship and went back to what felt safe. I took another corporate position, even though my body was literally rejecting the choice. I was outgrowing my clothes, outgrowing my skin, as if my physical form knew something my mind wasn't ready to admit.

You know that feeling, right? When everything looks good on paper, but something inside you is screaming, "Not this!"? When you're successful by every external measure, but you feel like you're slowly disappearing?

That's where I was. Shrinking myself to fit into structures I'd long since outgrown, telling myself it was strategy when it was really just fear. Someone else's fear, and we will explore that later in the book.

Here's the thing about ignoring good advice from people you trust: It doesn't make the truth go away. It just makes you more uncomfortable until you finally listen. While I was forcing myself to fit where everyone said I belonged, I found myself writing *Trust in Action*, ironically, as a way to learn to trust myself enough to leave.

Two years later, when I finally found the courage to step away and step into the LLC I started years earlier so I could do my own thing, I thought I'd cracked the code. I had the trust model figured out. I was helping leaders understand how trust moves organizations forward. But something kept nagging at me.

I could see it in every boardroom I walked into. The hesitation. The endless "let's think about this more" conversations. The half-hearted attempts at innovation that died in committee. These weren't bad leaders. They were capable, experienced people who genuinely wanted to create change.

But they were stuck.

And so was I, if I'm being honest. Because while I'd figured out trust, I was still dancing around something bigger. Something that lived in that uncomfortable space between knowing what needs to happen and actually making it happen.

That space is called risk.

Not risk like your compliance officer talks about it. Not risk like a spreadsheet full of likelihood and impact scores. I'm talking about the actual human experience of risk. That moment when you're standing at the edge of what you know, looking across at what's possible, wondering if you've got what it takes to make the jump.

Here's what I finally understood: Risk isn't the enemy. It's an invitation. It's the space between the Land of Now and the Land of Next, between who you are and who you're becoming, between the comfortable and the necessary.

And most of us have been taught to see that space as a danger zone instead of a design space. Think about it. How many times have you had a brilliant idea, felt the excitement of possibility, and then talked yourself out of it? How many innovations have died in your organization not because they weren't good ideas, but because the risk felt too big, too uncertain, too much?

I spent years watching leaders, myself included, get trapped in what I call oscillation: that endless loop of planning, analyzing, discussing, and replanning that feels like progress but delivers only delay. In oscillation, we mistake motion for movement, activity for action.

But here's what I learned from my own journey, from working with leaders across industries, from watching some succeed spectacularly while others stayed stuck: The leaders who thrive aren't the ones who eliminate risk. They're the ones who've learned to dance with it. They understand something fundamental that most of us miss: Risk isn't what's in the way. It *is* the way.

That's what this book is about. Not theoretical risk management, but the real, messy, human work of crossing the threshold from where you are to where you want to go. I'm going to show you a model I've developed called **Face, Frame, Forward**:

Face is about honest acknowledgment. It means that you see what's actually there instead of what you hope or fear might be there. It's the difference between external uncertainty and internal anxiety.

Frame is about meaning-making. This step takes what you've faced and puts it into context through your purpose, values, and vision. This is where risk transforms from exposure to opportunity.

Forward is about intelligent and informed action. It is when you move with clarity and conviction even when the path ahead isn't completely mapped out. This is courageous progress, carrying both the weight and the responsibility of moving forward. You'll see how this plays out in real situations, from my own journey leaving corporate life to build something new, to organizations that have transformed themselves by reframing challenges as competitive advantages. You'll discover why the most successful companies treat risk not as an obstacle to innovation, but as the very medium through which they navigate toward their future.

And listen, I'm not sharing this as someone who's got it all figured out. I'm sharing it as someone who finally stopped waiting for the fear to go away and started moving forward anyway.

Someone who has learned that being fearless isn't the goal. I strive to be fearFULL: full of conviction, clarity, and self-trust.

If you picked up this book, I'm guessing something in your life doesn't fit the way it used to. Maybe you've outgrown a role, a story, a system. Maybe you're feeling that same tension I felt, that low hum of "not this," that ache for "what's next." You're not alone. And you don't have to wait until you feel completely ready.

This book is for leaders who understand that in a world of constant change, the biggest risk isn't taking chances. It's standing still while others venture into tomorrow. This is a book for anyone ready to step into their next chapter not because it's safe, but because it's necessary.

Because here's the truth Angela helped me see, the truth she hammered into me until I finally listened: You can't go back to companies and situations that were never designed for who you're meant to become. You can't keep shrinking yourself to fit spaces you've outgrown. As Angela helped me see so clearly, we're born to build, not to fit into someone else's system. And definitely not to contort ourselves to meet expectations we've already surpassed.

Next starts here.

The old structures, the old ways of thinking about risk, the old patterns of oscillation, they're not serving us anymore. They're not serving our organizations, our communities, or our planet. The things we've come to rely on have fallen around us, and the only way forward is to stop trying to repair what's broken and start building what's needed.

That's not just my story. It's our collective challenge. And risk isn't our obstacle in that work; it is our way forward. Welcome to the gap. Let's build what's next. The next move is yours.

PART 1

Risk

Risk is often misunderstood, avoided, or treated like something to eliminate. This section invites you to see risk for what it really is, a gap between where you are and where you want to be.

Before we can navigate it, we have to face it with honesty and clarity. We've been taught to treat risk as a red flag, a threat to control, or a problem to be managed into submission. Entire systems are built around minimizing, containing, or outsourcing it. As a result, too many organizations stay stuck in neutral. "Wait and see" has become the new pandemic of leadership and is what I consider one of the greatest dangers today: hesitation that turns into inaction.

In Part I, we examine the core problem: our outdated perception of and relationship with risk. We've confused inaction with safety and control with clarity. We tell ourselves we are being prudent, when in reality we are often being passive. In a world where complexity and disruption are constants, that mindset no longer serves us. It limits innovation, erodes relevance, and weakens trust. The organizational cost is strategic and more importantly, culture. Teams begin to disengage. Leaders second-guess decisions. Opportunities slip by while organizations stay busy managing yesterday's problems.

Each chapter in Part I reveals how fear-based reflexes create the illusion of stability while quietly draining forward energy. We'll confront the myths around risk, unpack the leadership patterns that reinforce hesitation, and name the behaviors that keep teams stuck in analysis, avoidance, and indecision. We will examine external pressures like market volatility and regulatory change while also looking at internal systems, mental models, and organizational cultures that reinforce deeply embedded scripts we follow without question.

Before we can transform risk into opportunity, we must first be willing to see it for what it is and what it's not. Part I asks us to look at risk with new eyes, challenge the assumptions we've inherited, and begin to build the mindset shift that makes everything that follows possible.

1

The Risk *of* Risk is Risk

"We don't see things as they are, we see them as we are."

—Anaïs Nin, diarist and essayist

Refuse the Reflex

You are moving fast toward a new idea, a sharper strategy, a direction you have never taken before. Then suddenly, it appears: risk. And without even realizing it, you hesitate. You slow down. You second-guess your instincts. Not because you have fully assessed the danger, but because you have been taught to treat risk as something to avoid, rather than something to examine.

We have been conditioned to treat the word *risk* as a red

light. It triggers a deep and nearly unconscious response for us to stop, wait, protect, delay. We shift into a mode that prefers caution over possibility. We ask for more information, more certainty, more time. And yet, the very act of hesitating may be what places us most at risk.

What if the real danger is not the risks themselves, but the way we relate to them? When we allow fear to dictate our actions and let the possibility of failure stop us from moving forward, we create the outcome we most fear. We drift into irrelevance, lose momentum, miss out on innovation, and watch others move toward a future we are too afraid to explore.

See Past 'Stop'

From the classroom to the boardroom, we are taught not to make mistakes. The systems we operate within, from educational grading rubrics to corporate performance reviews, reward safety and consistency far more than experimentation and boldness. The message is simple: Avoid being the one who gets it wrong.

As a result, we end up managing risk into something that looks neat and tidy but lacks ambition. We strip away the uncertainty until the idea feels safe. But by the time it does, it has also lost its edge.

Think about the last time someone in a meeting said, "That feels risky." Most people likely nodded, and that was the end of the conversation. There was no deeper analysis, no curiosity, no discussion of what risk might also unlock or what staying still might cost.

I have seen this pattern over and over. In one executive

discussion, a forward-looking climate initiative was abandoned. Not because it lacked feasibility, or financial logic, or scientific support, but simply because someone said it might be too risky. No one had defined the actual risk. No one had even asked the right questions. They simply accepted the idea that the presence of risk was reason enough to stop.

Ironically, the decision to avoid that risk created a new and much larger one. While that company stood still, its competitors advanced. As they did, they changed the standard the laggards in that industry would later be judged against.

The Hamster Wheel

Why do we stay in this pattern? The answer is simple. We are caught in circular logic that feels safe even though it stifles progress. We tell ourselves:

"We didn't take the risk because it was risky."
"We trust this path because we chose it, and we chose it because we trust it."
"Risk protects us." (instead of asking whether it is actually holding us back)

This kind of thinking mimics logic but masks fear. It prevents forward motion while giving the illusion of good judgment.

At AstraZeneca, when I was leading our environmental strategy, this loop was everywhere. Net zero, the commitment to eliminate or balance out all greenhouse gas emissions across operations and supply chains, was seen as admirable, but not practical. We kept hearing that the data was not ready, that the technology was still developing, that other companies were not moving yet. Each objection, on its own, sounded reasonable. Together, they formed a perfect circle that would trap us in preparation indefinitely.

To break free, I asked our scientists to trust what they knew was possible. They were among the first in the world to take serious steps toward a credible net-zero path. No one else had shown the way, so they became the way. The risk did not disappear, but it stopped being the reason to stay still. It became the reason to move.

The Acceleration Gap

Martec's Law, created by marketing technologist Scott Brinker, states that technology changes exponentially, while organizations change logarithmically. I would take it one step further and say that individuals evolve faster than organizations, and organizations evolve faster than governments and regulations.

You can see this playing out in nearly every business. A mid-level marketing manager understands emerging platforms more deeply than the chief marketing officer. A frontline worker identifies ways to automate a process while executives cling to outdated systems. A customer service agent sees shifting consumer preferences in real time, even while senior leaders rely on reports from the previous quarter. The gap between personal capability and institutional agility is growing. And in every layer of that gap, risk aversion is what keeps progress stuck.

Martec's Law: technology
changes exponentially, while organizations
change logarithmically

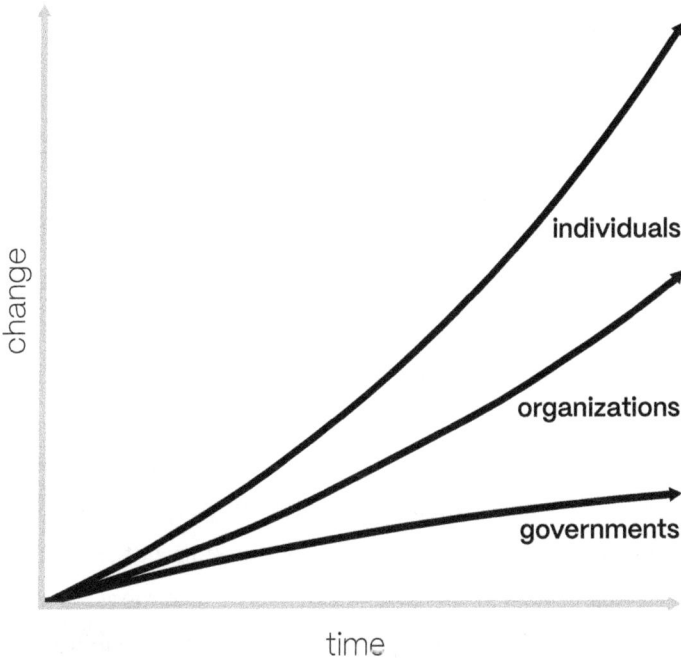

Scott Brinker, "Martec's Law: Technology Changes Exponentially, Organizations Change Logarithmically," *ChiefMartec.com* (blog), June 24, 2013, http://chiefmartec.com/2013/06 /martecs-law-technology-changes-exponentially-organizations-change-logarithmically/.

Two decades ago, when I entered the compliance world, the guidance was clear: Stay a few steps behind the risk line and you will avoid trouble. At the time, this approach seemed rational. Today, if you are still trailing behind the line of risk, you are no longer safe; you are obsolete. The world is moving fast. Innovation is moving faster. Compliance and regulation are often catching up, not leading. And the habit of treating compliance as the compass will not guide you toward relevance. It will keep you behind.

From Brakes to Navigation

When I first took on a global compliance role, I saw that many people still expected compliance to slow things down. That had been the model for years. Compliance was the brake pedal, the function that stopped bad decisions and prevented future liability. In a slower, more stable world, that was enough. But the world has changed. Slowing down is no longer the challenge; leaders now need help moving forward wisely, ethically, and with clarity.

So we stopped writing rules that only existed to say no. We started articulating principles that helped people say yes with confidence. Policies became tools for thinking, not restrictions for obedience. We invited complexity. We made room for judgment. We stopped shielding teams from responsibility and started preparing them to own it.

The job of compliance, at its best, is not to prevent progress. It is to protect trust while progress unfolds. It is to ensure movement is aligned with purpose.

At All Costs

We often learn from the stories of companies that failed to act, even when they saw what was coming. Blockbuster passed on buying Netflix. Kodak developed the first digital camera, then buried it. Nokia could not imagine a future without physical keypads. These decisions were not strategic miscalculations. They were moments where fear overpowered vision.

Even today's most innovative companies are not immune. Google helped develop the AI breakthroughs behind many of the tools we now use. Yet, because of internal hesitation, they delayed launching their own. OpenAI and Microsoft did not wait. The result was a shift in the market that Google had once shaped.

Meta invested heavily in virtual reality, rebranding the company and shifting strategy, but failed to fully engage with the AI revolution that unfolded in parallel. They chased the future they imagined, while missing the one already happening.

In the ESG space, many companies stood by, waiting for standards and regulations to be finalized. Meanwhile, companies like Unilever and Ørsted moved ahead, took bold steps, and helped define what responsible leadership looks like.

The pattern repeats itself. It is not a lack of insight or capital or talent. It is a failure to act with courage. It is oscillation disguised as preparation.

Oscillation versus Innovation

Oscillation is the illusion of forward movement. Teams stay busy, draft plans, revise strategies, and present updates. Yet nothing truly changes. The project stays in place, and energy slowly dissipates.

Innovation feels different. It moves. It does not wait for everything to be perfect. It does not eliminate risk; it learns from it. It generates real feedback, fueling internal alignment and unlocking transformational change.

Oscillation is the byproduct of a need for certainty. Innovation is the outcome of a willingness to move even when things are uncertain.

I have seen pilot programs die because no one wanted to take a clear stand. Everyone was waiting for someone else to make the first move. Eventually, timelines slipped. The team lost focus. The opportunity passed. The cost was not just a missed idea. The cost was belief in the work, in the team, and in the possibility of change.

The Mindset Divide

According to ISO 31000, the global benchmark for enterprise risk management, risk is defined as "the effect of uncertainty on objectives." This seemingly subtle shift, introduced in the 2018 update and reaffirmed in 2023, is profound. It reframes risk from being purely negative ("something to avoid") to something that can also be positive ("something to pursue"). A choice every organization must make: Do we manage risk through fear, or do we approach it with possibility in mind? This shift, even though very minor, started what I know to be the disruption in risk management.

Fear-driven teams ask, "What could go wrong?" and build systems to prevent mistakes. Their instinct is to contain, control, and correct. These environments often favor compliance over courage and preservation over progress.

Opportunity-driven teams ask, "What could become possible?" and design systems that make space for experimentation and growth. They understand that action and clarity, *not preservation and certainty*, create momentum, and that risk, when embraced thoughtfully, is the spark of innovation.

Both approaches see risk. Only one approach sees potential on the other side of it.

This shift is more than philosophical. It is strategic. A 2024 KPMG executive survey found that high-performing companies no longer treat risk as a compliance exercise. Instead, they see it as a strategic asset and a way to future-proof the organization by embedding agility and innovation into the heart of risk management. Or as the report puts it: "Organizations must completely embrace risk as an enabler—not just a hazard—to unlock growth in uncertainty."

In other words, the best companies design for risk instead of fear risk.

A New Day

What if risk is not an obstacle, but an entry point? What if it is not the thing blocking us from opportunity, but the territory we must move through to reach it? Risk is not what stands between us and progress. It is the path.

The greatest risk we face is not the possibility of failure. It is the habit of playing it safe. It is choosing the familiar over the meaningful. It is staying in the Land of Now because we are afraid of what it might take to get to the Land of Next. We do not need to eliminate risk. We need to learn how to move with it, through it, and beyond it.

Breaking the Cycle

Better thinking begins with better questions. For example, instead of asking, "What could go wrong?" ask, "What becomes possible?" Rather than focusing only on the risk of action, consider the cost of inaction. Challenge the assumption that the future will mirror the past and imagine it as a departure. Minor shifts in the language we use can significantly redefine the strategies we pursue. The way we frame questions reveals the limits of how we see the world, and how we see ourselves within it.

Tools like AI can help us test assumptions, validate concerns, and expose the blind spots in our thinking. But technology alone won't break the cycle. What's needed is a deeper willingness to think differently, open the conversation, and invite in people who don't share your point of view to challenge the comfort of consensus. Better thinking requires discomfort and the courage to listen when the answer isn't what you expected.

The rest of this book introduces the Face, Frame, Forward model, which provides a way to shift how we understand and engage with risk. Like any tool, it works only if we're willing to shift something deeper first: our relationship with risk itself. Risk is modeled through the questions we ask, the stories we tell, and the futures we are willing to imagine for ourselves and our organizations.

Risk of Risk

Here is the core insight I want you to carry forward: Risk is the distance between where you are and where you want to be. Every significant advance in business, in society, or in your own life has required someone to step into uncertainty. The people who shape the future are those willing to work with risk, learn from it, and lead through it.

Trying and failing is survivable. Never trying is not. The world is changing. Standing still is no longer safe. And the cost of hesitation is higher than we think.

The risk of risk is risk. Not because risk is inherently bad, but because the failure to engage with it may cost us the chance to become who we are meant to be.

2

Risk Redefined

"Risk is the gap between where you are and where you
want to go. Trust is the bridge. Fear is the fog."

—Jim Massey

We say we want innovation and that we admire it.
Companies proudly promote that they reward it.
Yet we rarely talk about what innovation actually
requires. Innovation demands movement. It asks us to step into
the unknown, to create without a guarantee, to move before the
map is drawn. It doesn't come with a manual, a blueprint, or a
promise that it will work. In fact, I'm convinced we don't even
share a common definition of innovation. Instead, it's become
a corporate virtue signal, a value companies claim but rarely
define. That is precisely where risk comes in.

What if the presence of risk doesn't mean we should stop, but that we're standing at the edge of something important? What if risk is actually an invitation?

Three Roads Converge

Here's the shift I want to offer. Risk is the space between where you are and where you want to go. Trust is the bridge you build to cross that space. Fear is the fog that makes it hard to see the other side.

We've all felt that fog. That creeping uncertainty. That sense that we're standing at the edge of something bold, yet all we can see are the outlines that make our view hazy, distorted, incomplete. In those moments, it's easy to pull back, to wait, and to pretend we're being prudent when really we're just afraid.

Here's the truth: You don't need full certainty to move. You need trust.

You need trust in your direction. Trust in your values. Trust in the people around you. And trust in yourself, that even if the outcome is unknown, the action still matters.

How Organizations Kill Innovation

It's not just individuals that hesitate. Systems do too. Most organizations reward what's safe. They don't intend to punish innovation, and yet they make it harder at every turn. The budgeting cycle doesn't account for experimentation. The approval process adds layers of friction. The cultural tone prizes perfection over progress. Innovation doesn't die because the idea is bad; it dies because the system makes it easier to say "not yet" than to say "let's try."

Trust erodes inside companies not by some big dramatic wave, but through a slow drip of learned hesitation. When teams learn that boldness is punished, they stop taking chances. When they're asked to cross the gap without a bridge, they instead think of job security and turn back. We have all experienced firsthand how culture drives this and how once that muscle atrophies, it takes real intention and time to rebuild it. The path forward gets swallowed by something quieter, heavier, and far more human than most leaders are willing to name.

The Fog of Fear

Fear doesn't always look like fear. Sometimes it looks like logic. It hides behind spreadsheets and "what if" scenarios. It dresses itself up as caution. But the result is the same: analysis paralysis.

Fear clouds the view. It makes the bridge seem narrower than it is. It makes the gap seem wider. It makes moving forward feel reckless instead of responsible. Fear leaves its mark in the regrets of opportunities lost while we waited for certainty that never came.

The cost of inaction isn't just missed opportunity. It's lost momentum, eroded relevance, and diminished trust in our teams and ourselves.

Crossing the Gap

The leaders who move don't have special tools. And they are not reckless. First-moving leaders are just committed to forward motion. They understand that risk is a signal, not a stop sign. They know that fog isn't a barrier; it's a condition. And they've learned how to build the bridge anyway. They move because the destination matters even though the way isn't clear. They move because not moving is the greater risk. They don't wait for permission. They move toward possibility.

Many leaders stay stuck because they've inherited stories about risk that no longer serve them. These myths show up as strategy, but they're rooted in fear. And unless we name them, they keep us from building the bridge. The following are examples of risk myths that hold us back:

Myth 1: "We need more data before we act."
Reality: Sometimes, our demand for more data is just fear in disguise. Data doesn't eliminate uncertainty; it just gives it shape.

Myth 2: "Risk is the opposite of responsibility."
Reality: The most responsible leaders often take the boldest risks because they're grounded in purpose, not fear.

Myth 3: "We'll act when things calm down."
Reality: Calm is the illusion. Complexity is the constant. Waiting too long is itself a risk.

If You Build It, They Will Walk It

We often think of innovation as a solo act. One person, one idea, one leap. The fact, though, is that most innovation scales because someone else made it safer to move. In most circumstances, the first leap is catalytic. It signals that movement is possible and survivable. When you build a bridge, you cross the gap while showing others how they can do the same.

That's exactly what happened when Matthias Gutzmann launched DPW (Digital Procurement World). In 2019, Matthias saw a problem most people ignored. Procurement was stuck. The industry, and therefore the function within companies, became risk-averse, slow, and disconnected from the startup world. Innovation was happening elsewhere, while procurement clung to legacy systems and recycled conferences. The gap between what was and what could be was wide, and no one was building a way across.

So Matthias left his job, moved back to Germany, and used his personal savings to create something new. The first DPW event in Amsterdam had no guarantee of success. But over four hundred procurement leaders from thirty-three countries showed up. Because someone had finally named the gap and built a platform for others to stand on. DPW built the stage on which a movement revolutionized an industry.

Startups gained visibility. Corporates gained courage. Partnerships emerged, like the collaboration between Roche and Axiom sparked through DPW Labs, which helped large organizations pilot new ideas without institutional inertia blocking the path.

DPW worked because it reframed risk. It showed that

innovation in procurement wasn't reckless; it was necessary. Matthias made it easier for everyone else to take a step by leaping into the fog and showing others there was a way. That's what trust does. It clears the fog for you and for the people watching.

Your Life's Work

I love this example from Matthias because it's a powerful illustration of what it means to leap into the fog. It shows that risk is about clarity of purpose and recognizing that the real danger is standing still in a system that no longer fits.

That's why this section is titled "Your Life's Work," not "Work-Life Balance." We've been taught to split our identities, to toggle between two selves, to walk a tightrope between professional and personal. This construct is a risk in itself. It distorts how we show up every single day. What if we stopped chasing balance? What if we simplified the question entirely, shifting from "How do I juggle it all?" to "What am I here to do?" When we choose to pursue our life's work, we begin to face a much more honest question. And that question isn't just "What's next?" It's "What becomes possible when we stop waiting—when we stop trying to fit into a broken structure and start showing up as who we really are?" Risk is the terrain of every meaningful pursuit, not a detour. You're not stuck because you're failing. You're standing still because the next path requires something different. You realize you need a new way to see, to move, to lead.

I spoke about this on *The Future of Trust* podcast. What began as a conversation about work-life balance quickly became something deeper. I shared a moment flying home from Indonesia, reflecting on how I was once again missing one of my kid's baseball games, missing *life*, because I was doing "the job." I felt like I had to choose between being present at work or present at home.

But then I said something that surprised even me: "I don't want work-life balance. I want to live my life's work." That shift wasn't about adding more hours or achieving equilibrium. It was about integration, being one whole person, everywhere. No masks. No split personas. Just me.

We've been told we must have two selves, professional and personal. We've been trained to believe that risk is only acceptable when it's impersonal, logical, contained. That's not how trust is built. It's not how purpose is lived.

When we compartmentalize, we fracture ourselves. When we unify, we build trust with others and with ourselves. That's what your life's work asks of you. You are expected to be present, not perfect. It asks you to risk being seen for who you really are. To stop waiting for the conditions to be ideal and to stop outsourcing your sense of readiness to someone else's expectations.

When we stop waiting for the fog to lift, when we choose to walk through it, we become the kind of leaders the future needs. We stop trying to master fear and start realizing the fear was never ours to carry. It was a story others told about how we should show up. Yet now we have a choice: Keep carrying that fear or show up, unmasked, authentic, and simply fulfill our life's works.

When purpose drives us as leaders, the "wait and see" game

ends. We stop standing at the edge, hoping the fog will lift. The Land of Next stops being a distant vision we watch from afar, and before we know it, the space around us is transformed. Once we cross the gap for ourselves, we see it more clearly: Our real work is building bridges for others.

This is exactly what some leaders and companies are doing now. They're neither waiting for certainty, nor asking for permission. Instead, they are moving forward with clarity, courage, and trust.

Stories from the Land of Next
Biotech – Moderna's mRNA Leap

Before COVID-19, Moderna was a relatively obscure biotech firm with no commercial product, only a bold bet: Messenger RNA technology could revolutionize medicine. Their platform had promise but was unproven at scale. Most legacy pharmaceutical companies opted for traditional vaccine approaches. Moderna leaned into the fog. They trusted the science and moved with urgency. The company's leaders understood that waiting for perfect conditions meant falling behind the pandemic curve. The risk was enormous—unprecedented scale-up, untested delivery infrastructure, and public scrutiny. But the reward? Historic. Moderna not only delivered one of the first authorized mRNA vaccines in record time; they validated a platform that will reshape biotech for decades. Their decision was not reckless. It was a leap of faith backed by trust—in the mission, in the science, and in the world they hoped to help heal.

Retail – IKEA's Circular Design Commitment

In 2021, IKEA announced its intention to become a fully circular business by 2030, a radical pivot from its mass-market, flat-pack past. This shift meant redesigning thousands of products to be repairable, recyclable, or remanufacturable. It also required rethinking how stores operate, how customers engage, and how global suppliers deliver. Internally, this was a culture shock. IKEA had built its success on affordable convenience. Now, it was telling the world, and its teams, that longevity and sustainability mattered more. In the end, the risk was the complexity of a brand transformation that touched everything, from the message IKEA shared with the world to the reinvention of a supply chain that had never been built before. Would loyal customers follow? Would sustainability scale profitably? IKEA moved anyway. It piloted buy-back programs in Europe, launched design labs for circularity, and retrained staff across functions. Over time, IKEA turned risk into relationship—strengthening trust with eco-conscious consumers, regulators, and next-gen workers who now see IKEA as a model of long-term integrity.[1]

Manufacturing – PepsiCo's AI–First Move

PepsiCo's journey into AI tells the story of a consumer goods company confronting risk tactically in code and hardware, and culturally in leadership itself. In 2025, it launched an

---

1 Sarah Butler, "Ikea UK to Buy Back Unwanted Furniture in Recycling Push," Guardian, May 5, 2021, https://www.theguardian.com/business/2021/may/05/ikea-uk-to-buy-back-unwanted-furniture-in-recycling-push.

enterprise-wide AI strategy that embedded intelligent tools into everything from flavor development to fleet logistics. Unlike some firms that limit AI to back-office automation, PepsiCo asked a different question: How can AI make our frontline teams better? They piloted tools that predicted shelf demand, routed trucks dynamically to reduce emissions, and used generative AI to improve call center scripts. But more importantly, they did so transparently. Each initiative was measured for real impact—cost, satisfaction, efficiency—and tied to employee training. The result? Trust. Across regions, teams began to see AI not as a replacement, but as an ally. And by building that internal bridge first, PepsiCo cleared the fog for everyone else watching.[1, 2]

Risk Redefined as a Practice

The stories you just read about Moderna, IKEA, and PepsiCo are real-world examples of what it looks like when leaders decide not to wait. They are evidence of what becomes possible when people act from conviction with clarity. They serve as a powerful reminder that the most important risk decisions are not confined to boardrooms or strategy decks; they are lived choices. They are made when we choose to move forward even when the

---

1 "PepsiCo and AWS Collaborate to Accelerate Digital Transformation," PepsiCo, May 7, 2025, https://www.pepsico.com/our-stories/press-release/pepsico-and-aws -collaborate-to-accelerate-digital-transformation05072025.

2 "PepsiCo Leverages Salesforce's Agentforce to Advance AI Agenda," PepsiCo, June 24, 2025, https://www.pepsico.com/our-stories/press-release/pepsico-leverages -salesforces-agentforce-to-advance-ai-agenda06242025.

outcome remains uncertain, when we decide to trust the clarity of our purpose more than the ambiguity of our fear.

That is the shift this chapter has been leading toward. Risk is not a problem to be solved or a signal to retreat. It is the space between where we are and where we hope to be. Redefining risk means we begin to see that space differently. It is not a gap to avoid. It is the landscape that separates what is from what could be, and when we choose to cross it, our courage turns ideas into action.

So now the question is no longer about case studies or theoretical models. Eventually, it comes down to what you are willing to face, what you are brave enough to frame, and what you are ready to do next. The fog is not abstract. The hesitation is real. And the bridge? That part is yours to build. No one is going to build it for you. The most powerful risk stories begin when someone decides to step in anyway and take action.

This is what it means to redefine risk as a daily, lived practice. It is not about waiting for the map to appear. It is about choosing to move with clarity. It is about building your own compass. And it is about trusting that movement matters, even if the journey is uncertain.

As you continue into Chapter 3, you'll dive deeper into the Face, Frame, Forward model. It is not a checklist, and it is not a formula. It is a way to navigate complexity with intention. Risk will show up again; it always does. This time, however, when it does, I want you to meet it with trust in your full self, grounded in clarity and ready to act.

3

Risk *in* Action

The Practice of Face, Frame, Forward

Before any meaningful action can take place, we must start with clarity. That means clearly and specifically naming the risk we are avoiding. In an environment full of noise—strategic priorities, shifting expectations, pressure to perform—it is easy to generalize risk or distract ourselves with surface-level concerns. Transformational leadership begins by facing the one thing that feels hardest to confront.

Slowing down to identify the real risk, whether personal, strategic, cultural, or operational, creates the foundation for forward movement. In this chapter, we move from naming the model to inhabiting it emotionally, intellectually, and operationally, building the muscles that come only through application to real decisions. What follows are a set of prompts designed to help you surface the tension you may be skirting, the bold step you have been postponing, or the truth you have been too busy to name.

What bold idea or next step are you hesitating to take, even though part of you knows it matters?

What do you keep postponing, not because it is the wrong thing, but because it is uncomfortable?

What feels at risk if you move forward? Is it your reputation? Control? Belonging?

What message are you sending by not acting? And is that the message you intend to send?

What matters enough to make movement worth it?

We cannot control every risk. But we can choose which one we are willing to face. And that choice is where leadership begins. Here, risk feels messy, disorienting, and emotionally charged. You do not know what to do yet, but you recognize something must be done. Leadership means noticing deeply, not moving quickly. You cannot manage what you will not face.

This simple idea is why I'm working to revolutionize risk assessment, not just as a tool, but as an actual philosophy. I've named the process and built a software platform called

Eastward, designed to help organizations operationalize risk as a product of leadership practice. It moves beyond static heat maps or annual reviews and instead embeds risk into the everyday rhythm of decision-making.

At its core, Eastward starts with a common language, one that cuts across organizational silos and dismantles subjective definitions. It provides a framework for leaders and their organizations to begin to face the risks that can propel the organization forward or threaten its license to operate.

One of the key ways we've done this is by developing a shared risk universe, focused on ten enterprise-level categories that consistently show up across modern organizations: strategic, people, governance, technology, compliance and fraud, operating, ESG, financial, reputational, and external.

No matter the industry sector, these ten categories surface again and again. Whether you're navigating clinical trials, digital transformation, geopolitical instability, or internal succession planning, the risk landscape is remarkably consistent. What changes is how we face it.

That's where Eastward comes in. Each category becomes a lens to detect, assess, and discuss risk in a clear, structured, and actionable way. Eastward supports leaders in evaluating likelihood, impact, and the effectiveness of controls, shifting the focus from "What are we afraid of?" to "What are we prepared for?" To lead in our ever-changing world, we must prepare to see both sides of risk: what could go wrong and what might become possible.

Lost in Translation

In many organizations, everyone is talking about risk, yet no one is really talking together. Compliance is worried about fraud, while commercial and R&D worry about relevance. Finance is forecasting revenue loss, while IT is securing the ever-changing technology. Each team is fluent in its own dialect of risk. Without a shared language, the conversations miss each other, and misalignment becomes the norm. That's why facing risk starts with one common foundation. A shared risk universe allows the entire organization to navigate complexity with consistency. I'm not saying every risk fits neatly into a box. I'm offering you a map before you can navigate the terrain.

Risk categories alone aren't enough. One of the biggest gaps we saw across industries was the lack of a consistent taxonomy, not just in how risk was labeled, but in how it was interpreted. Working with clients across sectors, we routinely found that different teams inside the same company used different terms, frameworks, and even scoring systems to assess risk. What one team flagged as "critical," another dismissed as "covered." What one leader saw as a compliance issue, another framed as a reputational threat.

So we built the Eastward risk universe from the ground up. We studied hundreds of companies, scraped public filings, analyzed ESG disclosures, interviewed risk professionals, and traced the language that showed up in both annual reports and boardroom conversations. These ten categories kept repeating as real-world reflections of how risk lives inside organizations today.

We also discovered something else. Traditional ERM

systems often miss what matters. Sustainability and ESG risks rarely show up in enterprise risk registers. People risks are ignored until they trigger a wave of resignations. Reputational risk is often treated like a PR problem instead of a leadership one. Risk was being managed and not meaningfully engaged. So we built a model designed for action as well as assurance. These categories are conversation starters, entry points to explore not just what might go wrong, but what's really at stake.

Here's how the model works: Every risk category becomes a lens. But for that lens to be useful, it must become **relational**. Not just scored and cataloged, but connected to real decisions. That's the shift. From naming risk in theory to engaging risk in practice. So the question isn't just "What category does this fall under?" It's:

- "What decision does this risk affect?"
- "What tension is it revealing?"
- "What's the consequence if we get this wrong?"

Without shared language, teams talk past each other. With it, they can see what matters, align, and act accordingly.

The Origin of Face, Frame, Forward

The Face, Frame, Forward model introduced in this book is rooted in theory and adapted based on the patterns I saw again and again inside real leadership teams. Whether preparing for regulatory shifts, product launches, or strategic pivots, the same behaviors showed up. When risk was left unnamed or talked about too vaguely, teams either froze, overreacted or, worst of all, stopped themselves from even discussing what was possible.

When leaders slowed down just enough to say what felt risky and why, everything changed. Better decisions emerged. Not because the fear disappeared, but because it was finally understood. Clarity replaced caution. Alignment replaced noise.

That's where Face, Frame, Forward began. It's not a step-by-step process. It's a leadership rhythm. A way to stay grounded when the stakes are high. And it starts, always, with the discipline to Face what's already in front of us.

A Tough Pill to Swallow

At McNeil Consumer Healthcare, a part of Johnson & Johnson, the brand identity was deeply tied to Tylenol, a trusted name in pain relief and a case study in both corporate crisis response and brand integrity. But in that culture, there was also an unspoken truth: Aspirin was the enemy. Generations of employees had internalized the idea that acetaminophen was special because it was better, safer, and more responsible. Aspirin, by contrast, had been painted as outdated or dangerous.

So when I was asked to help bring the St. Joseph Aspirin product into the company, I realize now that what I thought was a marketing challenge was really the work of addressing a cultural risk. Many employees felt as if I were walking into the organization and telling them their baby was ugly.

The world outside the company was changing along with the science. The benefit of low-dose aspirin in heart health was now widely accepted by the medical community. The product clearly had value. The real question was whether we had the courage to face our own internal bias and shift the story. We were not wrong before. We were not dishonest. But we were incomplete. And to evolve, we had to face that gap.

This required me to go on a roadshow, engaging with the people who had built the company and inviting them into the next stage of transformation. We named the tension. We acknowledged that something we had once dismissed could now expand our ability to serve patients. Facing the risk meant honoring the past while stepping more fully into the present and preparing for what comes next.

Mirror, Mirror

Facing is about recognizing rather than reacting. The discipline of naming the risk, the one that keeps you up at night, not just the convenient one, is where transformation starts. This step is about seeing the problem clearly enough that your next move is grounded in truth rather than assumption. The following prompts are meant to serve as invitations to slow down, to sit with discomfort, to hold the mirror a little longer before stepping into the fog of action. Only then can you reframe with integrity.

What story are you telling yourself about this risk? And is it true?

What are you avoiding by staying vague?

Who else is impacted by the risk you are hesitant to face?

What clarity might emerge if you said it out loud?

Naming the risk does not make it easier. It makes it real and therefore allows a leader to lead.

Frame the Fog

In the center of the risk model, what I often refer to as the risk bowtie, chaos begins to take shape. This is where convergence happens. You begin to make sense of the mess by filtering the risk you face through what matters most. This isn't a quick get-it-done exercise. Here, context is everything.

You weigh your values, goals, and realities. You bring strategy and story together. The work is to understand fear rather than eliminate it, creating frames that focus on mental models and meaning to help guide action. Framing gives risk meaning. It clears the fog and reveals the picture you need to see.

When Product and Purpose Collide

At AstraZeneca, one of our most commercially successful products was an inhaler used by millions of patients for respiratory disease. But as we deepened our environmental strategy, something became clear: The propellant used in that inhaler contributed to greenhouse gas emissions and ozone depletion. This wasn't just a reputational risk; it hit many other areas as well, including environmental, strategic and operations.

If we continued producing that inhaler as is, we risked being a company simultaneously treating and worsening the same disease. Framed as a cost issue, the investment to reformulate the product seemed unjustifiable. When we reframed it as a health issue—recognizing that our product, while therapeutic, was also part of the problem—everything shifted.

We stopped asking, "Can we afford to fix this?" and started asking, "Can we afford not to?" That frame created executive alignment, unlocked investment, and reminded us that credibility in science also means owning what the science shows, even when it's about your own product. Framing, in this case, was a matter of purpose.

Forward With Trust

Now, movement becomes possible because the path has shape. You have faced what was unspoken. You have framed what matters. And now, you step forward with clarity, intention, and trust. This is where courage is activated. The decision to move despite fear. Action becomes a deliberate expression of values, priorities, and leadership. It reinforces a key insight: Action without clarity is chaos. Action with clarity is courage. You move because the moment calls for it, and inaction is no longer acceptable.

All in Favor?

We often associate forward movement with broad organizational alignment. But some of the most transformative actions begin with a single, committed individual. In my experience, the decision to build momentum rarely comes with a unanimous vote. It comes from clarity and conviction.

One biotech company I worked with faced mounting pressure to delay a clinical development project until the next fiscal cycle. Budgets were tight. Priorities were shifting. But one mid-level program leader made the case that even small forward progress—securing a critical vendor, scheduling preliminary ethics reviews—would preserve momentum and signal intent. She moved first. That one step clarified the team's direction and catalyzed broader support. Waiting wasn't safer. It was riskier. When teams see movement aligned with values, not perfection, they follow. This is how we stop the oscillation, build resilience, and put risk in action.

Risk: Creating clarity for action

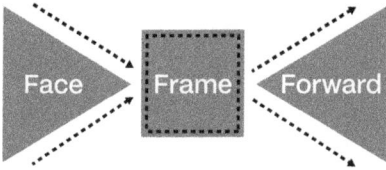

When leaders use the **Face, Frame, Forward** method, risk shifts from being an obstacle in the way to becoming the way forward. It serves as an invitation to innovation for leaders and organizations alike, moving us from where we are to where we need to be next.

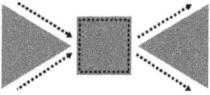

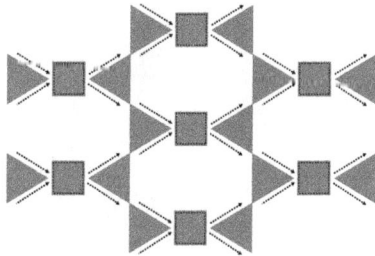

Leader   **Organization**

PART 2

Leader's Guide *to* Risk

Having named the problem, we now shift into the solution. I created this framework to be a leadership guide to risk. It is not meant to be a checklist, a new process, or a set of rigid steps designed to control uncertainty. Having been on the frontlines of leadership, I knew the importance of having something I could use in real time. Face, Frame, Forward is a repeatable, human practice, a leadership rhythm that helps individuals and organizations engage with risk consciously, creatively, and courageously.

As an executive and a leader of people for more than twenty-five years, I often found myself in situations where I needed something practical, something I could recall in the moment. I needed a resource that could help me decode what was happening beneath the surface of a team dynamic or a stalled decision. I didn't need another framework for the bookshelf. I needed a tool I could actually use in real conversations.

Just as the **Can, Care, Do** model helped me understand trust, where it breaks down, and how to build it, I needed something for risk. Something fast, simple, memorable. A way to make sense of the invisible forces that shape behavior when someone says, "We've never done that before," or "That sounds like it could be a gray area." What could easily be mistaken for just passing comments are really signals that fear, legacy thinking, or institutional caution might be shaping the path forward more than clarity or purpose. I needed a way to lead others through the gap, helping them face and frame risk so they, their teams, and their organizations could move forward.

That search for clarity is what gave shape to the risk model you're about to explore.

These chapters offer language for what often feels intangible. You will find tools to escape the oscillation trap, navigate competing polarities, and move decisively even when the path ahead is unclear. The model helps you build the leadership muscle to act when the ground is shifting under you and the stakes are high. Risk is leadership. How we face it, frame it, and move forward through it will determine whether we hold back or step boldly into what comes next.

4

Face *the* Music

The Real Risk is Not Knowing What You're Risking

There's a moment the music starts and you realize you have to move. It's not always graceful. Sometimes it's awkward, and the beat is there waiting, along with the decision: Will you face it, or will you just stand still?

Risk is like that. It plays in the background of every major decision. Sometimes it's a steady drumbeat that's subtle but persistent. Other times, it crashes in like a cymbal as a sharp, undeniable, impossible-to-ignore emphasis. Whether you hear it or not, the rhythm is always there. The real question is whether you're paying attention to it or doing everything you can so you don't see the play button.

Most organizations try to "see no evil." They push risk into frameworks instead of conversations. They schedule risk reviews once a year instead of building risk-sensing muscles into everyday decisions. They block their sight with performance dashboards while ignoring the signals that something fundamental is shifting underneath.

We say we want to be proactive, but we wait for the annual strategy offsite. We say we value foresight, but we benchmark yesterday's risks. We say we're future-ready, but we organize our risk assessments around categories from a decade ago and then act surprised when the rapidly changing world refuses to fit inside them. Facing risk is about reacting in real time because we are listening more deeply. It's about tuning in to the signals you've trained yourself to ignore because they're inconvenient, uncomfortable, or unfamiliar. Face is the first part of our model because you can't frame what you refuse to see, and you can't move forward if you won't pause long enough to tell the difference between what's real and what's imagined.

About Face

Recently, I worked with a leadership team preparing to launch their company's first formal impact strategy. On paper, they had done everything required to meet regulatory expectations: They had assessed their environmental, social, and governance risks; aligned with stakeholder priorities; and completed the necessary reporting steps. But once we began to connect that work to the broader corporate strategy, two uncomfortable truths emerged. First, there wasn't a clearly defined corporate strategy. Second, the organization had developed a culture where nearly every decision was filtered through a single question: "Is this required?"

That mindset didn't come from nowhere. Years earlier, the company had experienced significant legal challenges tied to the actions of a few bad actors. Though those individuals were long gone, the residue of that era remained. Out of caution, leadership began to rely on legal, regulatory, or other external mandates as the guiding light for action. Over time, that approach became ingrained into the company's decision-making. Whether decisions were about operations, innovation, or social responsibility, the instinct was to do only what was mandated and nothing more.

That caution soon bled into performance. Revenue targets were missed; creativity waned. And while the board pushed for a bold new direction, the organization struggled to break free from its self-imposed limits. What started as protection had become a constraint. That's when our work shifted. We realized we were delivering an impact strategy that was also helping the organization name what had gone unnamed: The absence of a unifying corporate narrative and the presence of a risk-averse culture that was no longer serving them. Once the leadership team could say it out loud, alignment began. The strategy work became a mirror reflecting both what was holding them back and what was required to move forward. That was the moment things started to shift. A transformation that started when the leaders faced the fact that risk-aversion had seeped into the culture, shaping nearly every facet of decision-making.

Reflex to Readiness

In many companies, risk is still treated like a reaction to be cataloged, scored, and controlled. When something goes wrong, we run the drills, complete the forms, and hold the lessons-learned session. We then move on, assuming the box has been checked. In a world of constant change, risk does not just show up once; it is continuous. And if risk is always moving, we can't afford to respond only after the fact. We have to face it.

Facing risk means more than identifying threats or ranking them on a heat map. It means acknowledging what is uncomfortable, unknown, or inconvenient before the impact hits. The shift begins when we stop treating risk like an event and start treating it like a signal. A signal to pause, to pay attention, to ask what is changing and how we need to adapt. Facing risk builds readiness to address the fear, not eliminate it, moving us from knee-jerk to know-how.

In Plain Sight

Facing risk begins with how we talk about it. Language either opens up awareness or shuts it down. A few practical shifts:

- Replace vague labels like "strategic risk" with specificity: "We might lose relevance with our target audience."

- Trade judgment for clarity: "We're unclear how this decision aligns with our purpose."

- Avoid euphemisms that obscure the truth: "We're navigating challenges" often hides "We're losing trust."

And watch for these common avoidance patterns:

- **Delay through Data**: Asking for more analysis when what's needed is a real conversation.

- **Confusing Activity with Progress**: Staying busy to avoid ambiguity.

- **Overcontrol**: Managing risk through micromanagement instead of collective clarity.

These are the habits that bury risk until it becomes a crisis. The goal is to build fluency into our leadership so that risk becomes core to how we lead, not something we tiptoe around. And that fluency has to live at both system and individual leadership levels: When leaders avoid risk personally, organizations often reflect that avoidance. And when systems punish honesty, even courageous leaders hold back. Building a risk-aware culture starts with clarity at both levels, what we model as individuals, and what we make possible through the structures we lead.

System and Self

Risk lives in culture and in people. It shows up in the decisions leaders delay, in the meetings people avoid, and in the silence that follows a risky suggestion. Risk is shaped by how power is used, how trust is earned, and how people interact when no one's watching. That's why our enterprise framework isn't just about categories and controls. It's about behavior.

Every organizational risk has a personal counterpart. The

risks that stall organizations often mirror the ones that constrain leaders. What is key, and often overlooked, is that risk flows in both directions. It does not just press down from the enterprise into leaders. It also flows upward and outward as leaders bring their own pressures back into the enterprise. The personal dynamics of leaders can shape and even destabilize the very categories they are meant to manage. Because we as humans are part of multiple systems—families, schools, communities, faith traditions—we carry those learned patterns of navigating risk with us into our leadership.

Consider a few examples. A leader who lacks clarity creates strategic drift across the system. An overwhelmed leader contributes to cracks in operating discipline. Avoidance at the personal level opens the door to compliance failures. And when leaders protect their own image instead of engaging risk directly, reputational trust across the enterprise weakens.

Similarly, strategic drift or a lack of clarity in the organization will impact a leader's evenings, weekends, and family life. An understaffed and overwhelmed organization will contribute to cracks in the personal capacity and performance discipline of individual leaders. Compliance failures may tempt or corner those responsible into choices that stretch or break their integrity. When organizations introduce risk into their systems at the expense of addressing it head on, leaders are left holding the bag of no-win decisions that threaten their integrity, resolve, and ability to take action.

Self risk does not represent character flaws or leadership defects. These are reflections of risk made personal. And when leaders and organizations face them clearly, we give our teams permission to do the same, which drives both organizational and personal effectiveness.

System risk and self risk are never separate. They mirror, reinforce, and at times undermine one another. The dynamic between system and self plays out every day inside organizations when the pressures leaders carry shape the risks their enterprises face, and when organizational risks press back into individual choices.

Facing AI Bias: IBM's Strategic Retreat

In 2020, IBM became the first major tech company to fully exit the general-purpose facial recognition business. The company pivoted and in doing so, to a principled stand. Citing the potential misuse of AI for mass surveillance and racial profiling, IBM CEO Arvind Krishna called on Congress to adopt federal regulation and oversight of facial recognition tools. This came amid mounting research, including the landmark "Gender Shades" study, which showed facial recognition tools underperformed significantly for individuals with darker skin tones.

IBM's leadership acknowledged that even advanced technology can reinforce societal inequities when risks are not adequately faced. By walking away from a lucrative business line, IBM signaled that the ethical risk outweighed the commercial reward. As Krishna put it, "We will not condone uses of any technology . . . for mass surveillance, racial profiling, violations of basic human rights and freedoms."

The company faced what was uncomfortable: a clear line of accountability.

Facing Incentive Risk: Wells Fargo and Misaligned Culture

In 2016, Wells Fargo became a case study in how incentive structures can produce systemic risk. The scandal involved employees who created millions of unauthorized accounts to meet aggressive cross-selling targets. It was the product of a culture that incentivized results without regard for the method of achieving them.

Despite warnings from internal risk officers, the system persisted for years. But eventually, public scrutiny forced the board and leadership to reckon with the truth: The incentive structure itself was the risk.

Reforms followed, including clawback provisions, changes to compensation, and the removal of senior executives. Even with these changes, the damage had been done to the organization's reputation, employee morale, and stakeholder trust. This was a leadership failure to face how deeply culture and compensation shape risk behavior.

The Essence of Face

To face risk is to tell the truth about what's there, even when it's uncomfortable. It's the discipline of naming what others would rather ignore in order to create clarity and alignment. When we have both clarity and alignment, we can move forward boldly and together. You can't move in harmony if you're still pretending there's no music to hear.

Naming the risk is only the beginning. Once you've faced what's real, the next question is what it means. This is where framing begins, the essential work of assigning context, inter-preting impact, and aligning around what matters most. How we frame the risk will determine how we respond to it and what future we make possible.

5

Ready, Set, Frame

"The greatest weapon against stress is our ability
to choose one thought over another."

—William James

I n an age of accelerating change brought on by AI disruption, geopolitics, shifting regulations, and rising stakeholder expectations, risk lives in our daily decisions. That is why the challenge we face is to agree on what the risk means in the context of our day.

This is where framing comes in. Once dismissed as a soft skill, framing is the ability to determine whether we move, freeze, or fall behind. Two companies can face the same risk and respond in completely different ways, simply because they see it through different frames. And the most resilient organizations? They choose their frames with intention.

When the Earth Moves Under Your Strategy

"EU Delays Corporate Sustainability Reporting Directive Implementation"

—Financial Times, February 27, 2024, 6:43 AM GMT

I was having my morning coffee when the headline hit my phone. In an instant, months of strategic planning for dozens of clients shifted. The European Union's Corporate Sustainability Reporting Directive (CSRD)—a massive regulatory framework that would have required detailed ESG disclosures from thousands of companies—had been delayed indefinitely.

My phone started buzzing immediately. Clients who had been scrambling to prepare for compliance were suddenly asking: "Does this mean we can stop? Are we off the hook?"

That's when I realized we had a framing problem.

They were seeing this as binary: regulation on or regulation off. Risk present or risk absent. But the real world doesn't work that way. While the EU was pumping the brakes, California was accelerating. Australia was moving forward with its own standards. The UK was charting a different course entirely. The regulatory landscape hadn't disappeared. It had just become more complex. And the companies that understood this distinction were the ones that would thrive.

Context Changes Everything

In traditional risk management, we talk about impact. We offer scenarios that help leaders and organizations think about how severe the consequences would be if a risk occurred. We assign scores, create matrices, and rank everything from low to high. For decades, this has been the measure through which we evaluate our top-tier risks. The problem is that thinking about impact alone misses something crucial: meaning.

A $10 million loss means something very different to a startup than it does to a Fortune 500 company. A data breach means something different to a healthcare company than it does to a manufacturer. A leadership change means something different during growth than it does during transformation.

This is why framing is fundamentally different, broader, and more insightful versus an impact assessment. Impact asks, "How big is this?" Framing asks, "What does this mean to us?" When you frame risk properly, you're not just measuring exposure. You're determining significance based on your values, your strategy, and your aspirations and the potential impact to your various stakeholders.

ESG Reframed

Let me tell you what happened with that CSRD delay mentioned at the start of this chapter. While some companies celebrated what they saw as a reprieve, others used it as an opportunity to reframe their entire approach to sustainability reporting.

One client, a midsized manufacturing company, had initially viewed ESG compliance as a burden. Leaders saw ESG as an added expense, time-consuming, and distracting from their core business. When we reframed the question from "How do we comply?" to "How do we compete?" everything changed.

Instead of seeing sustainability metrics as regulatory overhead, they began seeing them as competitive intelligence. Instead of viewing carbon reporting as a cost center, they started seeing it as a pathway to operational efficiency. Instead of treating supply chain transparency as a liability exposure, they recognized it as a trust-building opportunity with vendors who were bringing innovative solutions to the business.

The regulatory delay didn't change their approach; it accelerated their implementation. They realized that waiting for mandates was actually the riskier strategy. Their competitors were still playing defense while they moved to offense.

The Framing Advantage

Leadership today requires we change how we react to risk. In January 2025, the *Financial Times* ran an analysis titled "CEOs need a mindset shift on growth." It cited a McKinsey study showing only 30% of firms were investing in new businesses despite volatility, and just 8% felt confident in their talent pipelines. The article warned that many executives had fallen into the trap of treating uncertainty as a stop sign.[1]

The *FT* quoted psychologist Geoff Trickey, noting that the real risk was not an external threat as typically viewed via

---

1 Anjli Raval, "CEOs Need a Mindset Shift on Growth," Financial Times, January 2025, https://www.ft.com/content/9ac5ac6a-4288-4750-95a6-7585b2771926.

risk assessment. It was leaders losing the confidence to act. The message is clear that risk doesn't just need analysis; it demands framing.

The article reinforces the need to shift our mindset so that we see volatility as a signal that invites action. It doesn't just point to an external reality; it speaks to the heart of the Eastward framework, which demonstrates that how we frame risk shapes the way we move through it. When leaders frame uncertainty as opportunity, they choose growth while others remain stalled.

Fuel for Change

The IBM 2025 CEO Study reinforces this point. While many CEOs acknowledge the promise of AI, only 28% feel their organizations are truly prepared to scale it. Yet, 64% admit that their investment in emerging technology is not driven by strategic clarity, but by the fear of falling behind.[1]

This is the paradox of modern leadership: Hesitation feels safe but breeds irrelevance. When fear becomes the driver, we don't make bold moves. Instead, we make reactive ones. We believe that we have missing information, and yet the gap is a shared frame.

The organizations that thrive don't wait for perfect clarity. They act with conviction based on strategic framing: What are we optimizing for? What do we risk if we act? What do we risk

---

1 "IBM Study: CEOs Double Down on AI While Navigating Enterprise Hurdles," IBM Newsroom, May 6, 2025, https://newsroom.ibm.com/2025-05-06-ibm-study -ceos-double-down-on-ai-while-navigating-enterprise-hurdles.

if we wait? Those who frame AI and innovation as catalysts for reinvention and not as obligations or cost centers are moving forward while others are still forming committees.

Questions That Change Everything

Effective framing comes down to three fundamental questions:

- **What values or goals are at stake?** This is the clarity that comes when values shift from what you say to what you do—right here, right now. When faced with a cybersecurity risk, a company that values transparency frames it differently than one that values control. When facing market disruption, a company that values innovation frames it differently than one that values stability.

- **What tension are we holding?** Every meaningful decision involves polarities— competing forces that can't be resolved by choosing one. Instead, both must be navigated over time. Speed versus safety. Growth versus sustainability. Innovation versus reliability. The frame you choose determines how you manage the tension and optimize both areas that must coexist.

- **How do we want to see this risk?** This is where ambition enters the picture. Are you framing this risk from a position of scarcity or abundance? From fear or opportunity? From where you are now or where you want and, even more boldly, need to be?

Here's where many organizations get stuck: They have different groups using different scales to evaluate the same risks. Finance sees everything through revenue impact. Legal sees everything through liability exposure. Operations sees everything through process disruption.

This creates chaos, not clarity. When each leader, function, and team member uses a different lens to evaluate impact, decision-making becomes fragmented. One group sees a risk as catastrophic. Another sees the same situation as manageable. The result is organizational whiplash of constantly shifting priorities, reactive firefighting, and leadership teams talking past each other in crisis moments.

I've watched leadership teams spend entire meetings debating the definition of "material risk," only to leave more confused than when they started. This is especially true anytime my dear colleagues from Legal step in, and even more so when there's an SEC attorney present, because there are very clear definitions of materiality when it comes to external reporting, and they will never (and should never) back down from the risk they hold in that space. The problem is applying a changing environment to rules that no longer keep up, leaving misalignment around what low, medium, or high impact really means.

And here's where many organizations get it wrong. They try to borrow someone else's definitions. They download an off-the-shelf risk matrix from a consulting firm, apply it without context, and expect it to bring clarity. When thresholds aren't calibrated to your business model, your financial structure, your stakeholder expectations, and your cultural risk appetite, even the best-designed frameworks will fail.

This is why I couldn't just create a framework. I had to build a software solution to support companies in thinking this way consistently, contextually, and in real time. In our model, we focus on consistency calibrated to context. The software adapts to the organization, not the other way around. We don't impose a rigid, one-size-fits-all sequence of steps. Instead, we force organizations to stay honest with their own culture, their own language, and their own risk appetite.

Why? The answer is simple.

For a startup, high financial risk may mean a single decision that threatens next month's runway. For a global pharmaceutical company, high financial risk might mean anything that moves quarterly earnings by more than 5%. The scale is different. The stakes are different. But the need for alignment is the same.

That's the tension we help resolve. Consistent structure without forcing uniform thresholds that ignore business reality. Flexibility without abandoning the discipline of shared language.

Whether you're making a decision about next year's budget or responding to a global crisis, clarity only comes when people are working from the same frame, in their context, with their thresholds aligned, intentional, and understood.

The Power of Reframing

The most powerful organizational frames can come from many places—a workshop, a calibration exercise, or, most decisively, a crisis. In 2017, when Hurricane Maria devastated Puerto Rico,

Johnson & Johnson faced one of the most challenging tests of its operational resilience. The hurricane crippled infrastructure across the territory, leaving most of it without power. However, J&J's manufacturing facilities continued operating, thanks to pre-installed backup generators that were part of their comprehensive risk management strategy.

Though in a state of emergency, the company's foresight, anticipation of environmental risks, and investment in infrastructure to mitigate them helped the company keep operating. J&J had recognized the growing threat of climate-related disasters and taken proactive steps to ensure their operations could withstand such events.

Their preparedness allowed them not only to maintain production but also to support the community. While other companies struggled to resume operations, J&J's facilities became a beacon of stability, providing essential medicines and support to Puerto Rico's healthcare system.

The financial cost of these investments was significant. But the reputational trust, employee engagement, and long-term business impact were immeasurable.

More importantly, it became a defining moment of organizational identity. J&J wasn't just a pharmaceutical company operating in Puerto Rico. It was a purpose-driven organization that showed up when it mattered most. This is what aligned framing looks like in action: decisions that align with long-term values, stakeholder trust, and organizational identity, not just today's bottom line.

Navigating Risk: From Polarity to Possibility

The most sophisticated framing recognizes that many risks exist in polarity that can't be eliminated, only navigated. Take the classic tension between security and innovation. You can't maximize both simultaneously, but you can't ignore either. The frame you choose determines how you hold this tension.

Some companies frame this as "How do we innovate safely?" Others frame it as "How do we secure our innovation?" The subtle difference in framing leads to dramatically different strategies.

Companies that frame security as an enabler of innovation invest in robust security infrastructure that allows for rapid experimentation. Companies that frame innovation as a threat to security create approval processes that slow everything down. Same polarity, different frame, different results.

The companies that understand this recognize that the future of corporate sustainability isn't dictated by any single regulatory body. It emerges from a complex web of local requirements, investor expectations, consumer demands, and competitive pressures. The frame for organizations like this shift from compliance to readiness. From "What do we have to do?" to "What do we need to do to keep operating?" This is the power of strategic framing. It helps you see around corners that others miss.

Organizations that build the capability to frame appropriately move from reacting to risk to proactively shaping how risks are understood and discussed. They create shared language around what matters most. They establish clear criteria for decision-making. They train leaders to ask better questions, not just find better answers. Most importantly, they recognize that framing is both an analytical and emotional process. The best risk frames integrate both head and heart—what the data says and what the purpose requires.

The California Test Case

Back to my ESG story: While many of my clients were still debating the implications of the EU's delay in finalizing its sustainability disclosure rules, California was quietly moving forward with its own environmental disclosure requirements. Unlike the federal approach, California isn't waiting for 100% agreement. Following the rigorous science on global heating and climate resilience, the state is establishing its own regulatory frame, setting the pace rather than following it. As of this writing, the laws are not finalized, and they remain the subject of ongoing legal and political challenges. The message is clear: Environmental action by organizations is a moving target and an ever-present risk for companies.

This moment is a perfect case study of Martec's Law in action. The rate of change continues to accelerate. Individuals adapt faster than businesses. Businesses adapt faster than laws and regulations. Period. That means expectations for corporate behavior are shifting rapidly. Most likely, those of us in leadership will be expected to operate at the speed of business, which will stay steps ahead of where the laws are at the time of our decisions.

That's a drastic shift from when I first started in compliance. Back then, I was trained to stay two steps behind the line of compliance, never crossing it, and never getting too close either. The goal was to minimize exposure, reduce risk, and make sure we were safely inside the guardrails.

Today, that mindset won't cut it. If your organization is still asking, "Is this legally required?" your adaptability has already started to lag. And from here on out, it always will. That's the gap we as leaders must learn to navigate. Here's the truth: By the time the law catches up to expected behavior, it's already too late to build the capabilities you need.

Regardless of the final wording of California's climate legislation, the direction of travel was clear long before the ink will ever dry. Companies now face a fundamental reality: They must understand the risk of environmental change and global heating, not just in terms of regulatory exposure, but in terms of their operational footprint and their contribution to that change.

That's why disclosure is no longer a "What if?" It's a "By when?"

At the time I wrote this, California had just passed two breakthrough climate laws—SB 253 and SB 261—that sent a powerful signal about environmental accountability. SB 253 requires all companies generating over $1 billion in annual revenue and doing business in California to disclose their Scope 1, 2, and 3 emissions, regardless of where they're headquartered. SB 261, known as the Climate-Related Financial Risk Act, extends reporting by requiring companies with over $500 million in revenue doing business in California to submit biennial climate-risk disclosures aligned with the TCFD framework. Together, these laws establish a de facto standard, not just for public companies, but for *any* large organization doing business in the state. And while both laws await final regulations from the California Air Resources Board, they're already shaping real-time decisions and signaling a shift from voluntary to mandatory ESG action.

One client realized they'd be affected, not because they were based in California, but because their biggest market was the state. Suddenly, "We'll wait for the SEC" was no longer a viable frame. They reframed the situation as a strategic wake-up call: Readiness wasn't a future state; it was now table stakes.

The companies that understood this recognized something bigger: The future of corporate sustainability wasn't going to be dictated by any single regulatory body. It was going to emerge from a complex web of local requirements, investor expectations, consumer demands, and competitive pressures—all moving faster than any single company could control.

The frame shifted from compliance to readiness. From "What do we have to do?" to "What do we want to be known for?"

That's the power of strategic framing. It helps you see around corners that others miss.

Create a Culture That Frames Risk Boldly

Organizations that frame risk well respond more effectively, and they shape the conversation from the start. They clarify what matters, define how decisions get made, and create an organization where leaders are equipped to surface the real questions that lead to the best answers.

Most importantly, they recognize that framing is both an analytical and an emotional process. The best risk frames integrate both head and heart, which means appreciating what the data says and what the purpose requires.

When the next unexpected risk emerges, and we all know it will, it won't be the organizations with the longest risk register that succeed. It will be the ones with the clearest sense of identity and the most aligned decision-making frames.

From Framing to Forward Movement

Framing risk properly doesn't eliminate uncertainty. It makes uncertainty workable. When you know what matters most, you can act with conviction, even when you don't have all the information. When a leader chooses the right frame, they're shaping corporate culture. They're sending a clear message: "This is who we are when it's hard."

This is how leaders balance organizational risk and leadership risk, the very tension we explored in Chapter 4, "Face." By balancing the risk to the business with the risk to themselves, they become the kind of leaders people follow—leaders with a point of view and the integrity to admit they don't have all the answers.

Companies that thrive in uncertainty are the companies that frame risk in service of their mission, their people, and their future. Frame is the step in this model that allows us to bring meaning to risk, align action with purpose, and create clarity in uncertainty. In the end, risk doesn't demand certainty. It demands perspective. Framing is how we answer.

6

Forward—The Way Through

"Don't wait for permission to do something bold.
If you're waiting, you're already behind."

—Whitney Wolfe Herd, founder of Bumble

Forward Isn't Reckless

Risk triggers and wants a reaction. It deserves only a response. Too often, leaders are conditioned to treat risk as something to avoid, mitigate, or manage. It's reflexive: See a threat, pull back. In a world that changes faster than our policies can keep up, that instinct is outdated, and the behavior was never right.

That is why we need a different solution. One that doesn't retract. One that moves us forward wisely, not recklessly. Forward is practiced discipline, and, once developed, it is the only way through to what we need to create next.

Progress comes from building the capacity to move with risk. I once had a coach who told me the old saying "practice makes perfect" wasn't quite right. He said, "Perfect practice makes perfect play." That idea stuck with me, not because I believe in perfection, but because it reframed practice as purposeful repetition. In today's world, perfection often impersonates certainty, and that's exactly what we must unlearn. Practice, instead, means showing up with intention, trying again and again, and learning in motion. The issue isn't fear. What we're often missing is the leadership reflex for navigating what we haven't seen before. We grew up in systems that rewarded subject matter mastery. Today, the most essential skill is the ability to build capacity in real time, to adapt while still in the middle of the unknown. Over time, that capacity becomes discipline.

Just as athletes train in uncertain conditions to build muscle memory, leaders must train in ambiguity to build motion. This isn't something we get to do once. The future is unknown all around us. So we must practice as often as we can. Forward becomes less of a leap of faith and more of a rhythm we learn to trust in ourselves. Once we do that, we are ready to lead, here and now and toward the Land of Next.

Defense isn't Enough

Traditional risk management is built on a defensive triad: Avoid, Mitigate, Manage

The logic is simple: If something looks risky, don't do it. If you must do it, reduce the impact. And if all else fails, control it tightly. This model assumes that risk is static and that the world will wait for us to decide. It treats risk like a flood and the job of leadership like stacking sandbags. For decades, this served leaders and their organizations because the rate of change wasn't beyond the collective organizational capacity.

This is no longer the case. According to McKinsey, the number of significant disruptions impacting companies, everything from geopolitical shocks to regulatory shifts and technological upheaval, has more than tripled over the past two decades. The frequency and intensity of external shocks are now outpacing most organizations' ability to react.

Let's look at how this plays out in real organizations. The examples below show how different risk responses to **avoid, mitigate, and manage** show up in practice. Alongside each one, you'll see the relevant **enterprise risk categories** from the Eastward framework, the AI-powered risk assessment program. These pairings reveal not only *how* companies respond to risk, but *which* risks they are actually engaging or failing to face. When we recognize the patterns, we can start to ask better questions about what kind of risk posture we're modeling, and whether it's moving us forward or holding us back.

Avoid → Reputational + ESG Risk

In 2023, several telehealth providers retracted or limited access to reproductive services, citing regulatory and reputational risk—even as patient demand continued to rise. By avoiding the space entirely, they ceded both market opportunity and leadership in digital care. This wasn't just a values misalignment; it was a reputational risk multiplied by ESG inaction. In the effort to avoid controversy, these companies forfeited trust, relevance, and impact.[1]

Mitigate → ESG + Operating Risk

In 2024, Tyson Foods was sued by the Environmental Working Group for promoting its "climate-smart" beef and net-zero plans without a credible emissions reduction strategy. The company responded with patchwork messaging adjustments but failed to transform its supply chain. This is a prime example of how multiple risks show up for organizations. In this case, the risk was both environmental and operational, and the mitigation effort itself became a liability. As scrutiny around greenwashing intensified, it exposed the cost of superficial fixes in place of systemic change.[2]

---

1 Julia Harte and Sharon Bernstein, "Some U.S. Abortion Pill Providers Curb Availability after Appeals Court Ruling," Reuters, April 13, 2023, https://www.reuters .com/legal/some-us-abortion-pill-providers-curb-availability-after-appeals-court -ruling-2023-04-13.

2 Leah Douglas, "Green Group Sues Tyson Foods for Allegedly False Climate Claims," Reuters, September 18, 2024, https://www.reuters.com/sustainability /climate-energy/green-group-sues-tyson-foods-allegedly-false-climate-claims -2024-09-18/.

Manage → Compliance & Fraud + Governance Risk

For decades, pharmaceutical companies have faced scrutiny over promotional speaker programs—sales-driven events where healthcare professionals discuss branded products, often with compensation and perks provided to clinician attendees. Despite repeated DOJ enforcement actions and a 2020 advisory labeling these programs high-risk, many companies continue to "manage" the risk rather than reimagine the model. Some firms updated training or added oversight, but the core behavior remains unchanged. Rather than investing in new forms of engagement, leaders have clung to legacy practices, inviting compliance exposure and governance failure in plain sight.[1,2]

We see these patterns in every organization: cautious, predictable, and increasingly costly. The old risk management models were built for a different time. They were designed for a world where risks were mostly known, threats moved at a manageable pace, and stability was the expectation. The focus was on containment, control, and compliance so leaders could keep risk inside the lines and make sure nothing spilled over.

That approach made sense when the environment allowed for it. For decades, it worked. It gave leaders and their teams

---

1 "Special Fraud Alert: Speaker Programs," U.S. Department of Health and Human Services, Office of Inspector General, November 2020, https://oig.hhs.gov/fraud/docs/alertsandbulletins/2020/SpecialFraudAlertSpeakerPrograms.pdf.

2 "Acting Manhattan U.S. Attorney Announces $678 Million Settlement of Fraud Lawsuit against Novartis Pharmaceuticals for Operating Sham Speaker Programs through Which It Paid Over $100 Million to Doctors to Unlawfully Induce Them to Prescribe Novartis Drugs," U.S. Department of Justice, U.S. Attorney's Office, Southern District of New York, July 1, 2020, https://www.justice.gov/usao-sdny/pr/acting-manhattan-us-attorney-announces-678-million-settlement-fraud-lawsuit-against.

a sense of order and predictability. It offered a clear playbook: identify the threat, contain the damage, and move on.

Today's risk landscape moves faster than our sandbags can hold. The volume, velocity, and interconnectedness of risks have outpaced the slow, defensive strategies of the past. We're no longer facing isolated incidents. We're navigating what the World Economic Forum now calls a *polycrisis*: a web of compounding, overlapping threats, from geopolitical instability and AI disruption to climate volatility and misinformation.

The WEF's 2024 report warns, "We are entering a period of heightened risk complexity, marked by uncertainty and the breakdown of trust in institutions." And that breakdown isn't abstract. It shows up in boardrooms, supply chains, talent pipelines, and public discourse. This shift creates a new kind of leadership challenge while simultaneously providing a new kind of leadership opportunity.[1]

Leaders today have to design risk practices that open space for pursuit, encourage bold decision-making, and build organizational muscle for adaptability. Risk management must now become a driver of innovation and progress. The goal has changed from shrinking the organization's risk exposure to zero. Instead, the goal of risk management is now to build capacity, clarity, and responsiveness so the organization can engage with risk in ways that create value.

This shift requires a new mindset that views risk as raw material for better decisions, stronger alignment, and faster learning.

---

1 Saadia Zahidi, "Preface," in *Global Risks Report 2024*, World Economic Forum, January 2024, https://www.weforum.org/publications/global-risks-report-2024 /in-full/.

It's about moving from protection to possibility, from hesitation to informed action, from reaction to intentional response. The organizations that will lead in this new era are the ones that build risk capacity as a competitive advantage. They will treat risk as a source of insight, energy, and strategic direction. They will survive disruption because they'll shape what comes next.

I'm so adamant about transforming risk management because of what's happening right now in boardrooms and C-suites across industries. Consider the leadership succession crisis that quietly erupted in 2024 and 2025. CEO turnover hit record highs, with hundreds of companies scrambling to fill top roles amid economic instability, AI disruption, and rising stakeholder pressure. Many of these organizations had no real plan. They hadn't prepared to avoid the risk, hadn't taken meaningful steps to mitigate it, and lacked the tools or alignment to manage it when it arrived.[1,2,3]

This is what strategic people risk looks like when it goes unacknowledged. It's both a talent issue and a failure of foresight, alignment, and leadership readiness. It's also the clearest signal we have that the old ways of managing risk aren't working. This

1 "New Records Set: CEO Exits Surge Post-Election in December 2024," Challenger, Gray & Christmas, January 2025, https://www.challengergray.com/blog/new-records-set-ceo-exits-surge-post-election-in-december-2024-2/.

2 Isla Binnie, "Global CEO Departures Hit Record High in 2024 amid Investor Pressure," Reuters, January 29, 2025, https://www.reuters.com/business/global-ceo-departures-hit-record-high-2024-amid-investor-pressure-2025-01-29/.

3 Callum Borchers, "Why More CEOs Are Heading for the Exit," *Wall Street Journal*, May 2025, https://www.wsj.com/lifestyle/careers/why-more-ceos-are-heading-for-the-exit-f8b23e1c.

moment demands more than governance. It demands vision, which requires facing what we've been avoiding.

The Paradoxical Path

"Top-performing CEOs are distinguishing themselves not by controlling ambiguity, but by navigating it—balancing short-term deliverables with long-term adaptability."

—IBM 2025 CEO Study

Most leaders fall into "either/or" traps: move fast or move safely, innovate or maintain stability, take risks or protect assets. But the most effective leaders embrace both/and thinking. They move fast *and* safely. They innovate and preserve. They protect and progress.

In complexity, binary logic breaks down. The more interconnected the world becomes, the more our decisions carry ripple effects. It's no longer a question of choosing sides. We, as leaders, must hold the tension of complex topics long enough to move with integrity. The essence of polarity thinking is recognizing that many tensions in leadership are not problems to be solved, but polarities to be navigated. Competing values require balance, not resolution.

We can see this across sectors: product teams shipping fast and prioritizing quality, organizations investing in AI and investing in people, leaders declaring vision and remaining open to change. In the apparel industry, for example, brands like Eileen Fisher have embraced automation in their supply chains while championing sustainable, artisan-crafted clothing. Their strategy combines operational efficiency with storytelling and ethics, demonstrating that embracing technology doesn't have to come at the expense of craft. This model contrasts with fast fashion's disposable mindset and provides a tangible example of navigating paradox with integrity.

We also see this at companies like Unilever, which have long held the tension between quarterly earnings and long-term impact. In 2024, despite pressure from activist investors to abandon ESG goals, Unilever doubled down by reaffirming its commitment to net-zero targets and sustainable sourcing. The CEO framed the decision not as ideology, but as strategy: "We serve shareholders best by serving future customers first."[1, 2]

We also see this tension at the heart of some of the biggest technological debates today. In 2024, as pressure mounted around AI safety, Google publicly recommitted to its AI Principles, deliberately slowing some releases to ensure greater oversight. That same year, Microsoft expanded its Responsible AI Council, embedding ethicists alongside engineers in key decision teams. The company made calculated decisions to trade short-term speed for long-term trust, knowing that public confidence in emerging technologies can be lost faster than it's gained.[3, 4]

Polarity thinking doesn't only live at the organizational level.

1 "Why We've Updated Our Climate Transition Action Plan," Unilever, May 2024, https://www.unilever.com/news/news-search/2024/why-weve-updated-our-climate-transition-action-plan/.

2 "Our Climate Transition Action Plan (CTAP)," Unilever, 2024–2025, https://www.unilever.com/sustainability/climate/our-climate-transition-action-plan/.

3 Prabhakar Raghavan, "Gemini Image Generation Got It Wrong. We'll Do Better," Google, February 2024, https://blog.google/products/gemini/gemini-image-generation-issue/.

4 "Google to Pause Gemini AI Model's Image Generation of People after Inaccuracies," Reuters, February 22, 2024, https://www.reuters.com/technology/google-pause-gemini-ai-models-image-generation-people-2024-02-22/.

It's deeply personal. As a leader, you're constantly asked to hold paradoxes, sometimes without even realizing it. You manage the risk of the business while also managing the risk to yourself as a leader. You're accountable for team outcomes and for your own professional reputation. You're expected to drive performance while also protecting people's well-being.

In every decision, you carry the tension between what the organization needs and what you, as a leader, are willing to risk. This is the ongoing leadership challenge: navigating the space between self and system, team and enterprise, short-term deliverables and long-term purpose. Holding paradox is the actual work of leadership, and this skill is what defines leadership in moments of uncertainty.

Some days, you're making choices that feel safe for the business but risky for you personally. Other days, you're taking a stand that feels aligned with your values but comes with organizational exposure. It is hard to remember that these are polarities to manage and not separate competing forces to eliminate. The goal is balance both and move through them with clarity, integrity, and strategic awareness.

Here are just a few examples of the paradoxes leaders face every day:

- Deliver results and care for people
- Set direction and stay open to change
- Act quickly and remain thoughtful
- Hold accountability and offer support
- Manage risk and create opportunity

The more skillfully you hold these tensions, the more trust you build with your team and with yourself. Polarities define what real-time leadership looks like today. This type of thinking has become a survival skill for leading in today's world.

As Brian Emerson and Kelly Lewis write in *Navigating Polarities*: "It relies on a way of being and doing that most of us were never taught. It requires that we pause and look inward to discover how old habits and hidden assumptions undermine the results we seek. It requires self-awareness, conscious choice, and courageous action."

The paradox is the path, and leaders who walk it develop range, resilience, and real authority.

That's what Forward demands. It's about moving through uncertainty with eyes wide open, aware of the trade-offs, grounded in your purpose, and ready to act. Every step forward carries both risk and opportunity. And the leaders who make the greatest impact are the ones willing to move anyway while holding the paradox, framing the risk, and choosing action with intention.

Certainty Is Overrated

The old model of leadership was built on the illusion of certainty. Leaders were expected to have an answer for everything, present a detailed and exact plan, and deliver clear, predictable outcomes that eliminated ambiguity. Confidence was measured in definitiveness. Authority was tied to having the "right" answer.

In today's world, that model crumbles, and often, so do

the leaders still trying to live inside it. The pace of change, the complexity of systems, and the interconnectedness of global risks make certainty a luxury no one can realistically afford. Information is incomplete, variables shift overnight, and what felt true yesterday may no longer apply tomorrow. This is the new reality for leaders and organizations.

Leaders today are called to navigate through ambiguity with clarity of intent and strength of perspective. It means taking action even when the full picture isn't available, because standing still is no longer a viable choice. The most valuable leadership skill in this environment is the ability to move forward while holding multiple competing truths. To make decisions with conviction, while staying open to change. To act with clarity, knowing that new information will emerge and adjustments will be required. It sounds like this: "We believe this strategy is right, and we're prepared to pivot." "We're investing in this technology, and preparing for its obsolescence."

Leadership today demands the ability to move forward with trust in your internal compass, even when the map is still being drawn. I experienced this in a very real way when I took my family to Antarctica. We left Ushuaia, the southernmost city in South America. I had initially wanted to fly. There was a plane option. But the family convinced me that there was only one true way to experience Antarctica: through Drake Passage. For those who don't know, Drake Passage is where three of the world's oceans meet. It can be incredibly turbulent. So turbulent, in fact, it's nicknamed Drake's Lake when it's calm or Drake's Shake when the waters are rough.

I researched every boat I could find, ultimately choosing

one with all the stabilizers available. On the way there, we were lucky. It was calm, and I could happily travel through Drake's Lake. On our way back, we weren't so fortunate. We experienced Drake's Shake. There were long stretches of time when we couldn't see anything beyond the forty- to fifty-foot swells. Yet we trusted the passage and those who were guiding us. Even though we couldn't always see, we knew we were going in the right direction.

That journey became a living metaphor for how I think about risk. On the way down, we were headed toward something unknown, a hidden world that few get to see. On the way back, we headed home to safety and to share the experience. In both directions, movement required trust in the vessel, the crew, and the direction. And here's the nuance. In the physical world, the distance between Ushuaia and Antarctica doesn't change. But in our world of technology, rapid innovation, and continuous disruption, the destination is not fixed. Every day we delay, every time we hesitate, the landscape shifts. The destination moves farther away, not just in time, but in relevance. The future doesn't ask for perfection. It requires progress.

When we face risk, frame it with intention, and choose to move through it, something shifts. We stop the oscillation and unlock the conditions for innovation. Forward begins with a decision and a willingness to step onto ground that feels uncertain and unsteady. The important distinction is that forward momentum is shaped by how we choose to move.

From Playing Defense to Practicing Risk

If *avoid*, *mitigate*, and *manage* are the language of defense, then Face, Frame, Forward is the language of practice. The facets of this model help us survive risk because we learn to move with it. They become disciplines, habits of leadership. The following examples illustrate how the practice of risk comes to life one habit at a time: facing it, framing it, and moving forward:

Face

To face risk is to look directly at what you've been conditioned to avoid. Not the sanitized version, the real risk. The one that threatens your relevance, reputation, or responsibility.

In 2023, after the collapse of Silicon Valley Bank shook the financial system, several regional banks were forced to confront their own vulnerabilities. While many tried to downplay similarities, First Republic Bank chose to face its structural risks head-on, holding emergency stakeholder meetings and collaborating transparently with regulators. Though the bank ultimately failed, its leadership's willingness to face reality helped stabilize the situation and protect customers.[1,2]

---

1 Janet L. Yellen, Jerome H. Powell, Martin J. Gruenberg, and Michael J. Hsu, "Joint Statement by the Department of the Treasury, Federal Reserve, and FDIC," U.S. Department of the Treasury, Board of Governors of the Federal Reserve System, and Federal Deposit Insurance Corporation, March 16, 2023, https://www.fdic.gov /news/press-releases/2023/pr23020.html.

2 "11 Banks Deposit into First Republic Bank," JPMorgan Chase, March 16, 2023, https://www.jpmorganchase.com/ir/news/2023/bank-to-make-uninsured-deposits -totaling-30-billion-into-first-republic-bank.

Frame

Framing is how we make sense of risk. It's the act of placing it in the right context: understanding what's truly at stake, what matters most, and what we're actually solving for.

In 2024, Google paused the rollout of its AI image generation tool after it produced inaccurate historical depictions. Instead of treating it as a technical bug, leadership reframed the problem: This wasn't a software issue; it was a trust issue. That shift changed how the company communicated with the public and recalibrated its internal priorities.[1,2]

Forward

Once risk is faced and framed, the question becomes "What now?"

In 2025, Patagonia began piloting a circular product model, offering lifetime repair credits and resale guarantees. It wasn't proven. Yet it was a step. The company moved forward because the purpose was clear. Forward is not about recklessness. It's about momentum with meaning and the clarity to take the next step, even without the full map.[3,4]

---

1 Prabhakar Raghavan, "Gemini Image Generation Got It Wrong. We'll Do Better," Google, February 2024, https://blog.google/products/gemini/gemini-image-generation-issue/.

2 "Google to Pause Gemini AI Model's Image Generation of People after Inaccuracies," Reuters, February 22, 2024, https://www.reuters.com/technology/google-pause-gemini-ai-models-image-generation-people-2024-02-22/.

3 "Ironclad Guarantee," Patagonia, https://help.patagonia.com/s/article/Ironclad-Guarantee.

4 "Worn Wear Trade-In," Patagonia, https://www.patagonia.com/trade-in/.

We often picture risk as something we are trapped in, like a maze with no clear way out. But risk is not a place. It is a gap we have to cross. The gap is the uncertainty, the unknown, the space between where we are and where we want to be. Trust is what allows us to build the bridge across that gap. It becomes the structure we walk on and the confidence we place in ourselves, our teams, and the choices we make.

That leaves us with one last variable: fear.

Fear is not fixed or predictable. It comes and goes, often rolling in when we least expect it. That is why I call it *the fog of fear*. It clouds our view, makes the gap look wider, and makes the bridge feel less stable. Yet the gap remains crossable. The bridge holds. And when we name the fog for what it is, we can keep moving forward.

As a leader who has relied on this model throughout most of my career, I can share one of its deepest truths:

The fog doesn't lift before we move.

It begins to lift *because* we move.

Progress comes when we stop waiting for perfect visibility and start trusting our ability to navigate as we go.

If you're waiting for certainty, you'll be waiting forever. The way through is forward. And forward begins like this:

- **Face** plants your feet at the edge of the gap.
- **Frame** helps you understand what lies between here and what's next.

- **Forward** is the step you take because you've chosen to move with intention, even if the way isn't clear.

The model gives us a way to move. Our challenge is that leadership doesn't unfold in neat frameworks or tidy diagrams. It unfolds in real life, under pressure, in motion, surrounded by competing voices, shrinking timelines, and impossible trade-offs. It unfolds in the fog.

That's where the real work begins. Not in the clarity of the page, but in the confusion of the moment. Because even when we know how to face risk, frame it, and move forward, something else always rises alongside. Something internal. Something that doesn't respond to logic or process.

Even with tools to navigate risk, tools alone are not enough in a world that demands faster, bolder decisions. Every action we take is influenced by three forces: risk, trust, and fear. They don't wait their turn. They compete for our attention. The leaders who will succeed in the future are the ones who've learned how to navigate all three at once.

PART 3

Acting *with* Clarity

Knowing how to navigate risk is one thing. Acting with clarity, especially when trust feels fragile and fear shows up, is something else entirely. This section is about turning intention into motion and learning that trust and fear are not opposites but interdependent forces. Trust enables us to face fear without being ruled by it, and fear, when seen clearly, can sharpen our sense of what matters most. Left unspoken, fear can take over. It turns into hesitation, avoidance, over-correction. It shows up in behavior before it ever shows up in a boardroom slide.

Where Part I revealed the problem and Part II offered the path, Part III is the proving ground where theory meets behavior, and where clarity must convert to action. In Part I, we exposed how fear distorts our perception of risk, keeping us stuck in loops of avoidance, overcontrol, or reactive urgency. In Part II, we introduced the frameworks. Now, in Part III, we apply, test, and build capacity. This is where the real stakes begin, where trust is stretched, fear shows up uninvited, and every step forward reveals what we are truly leading through. This is where Risk in Action moves from concept to a leadership habit.

Here, the personal and the organizational converge. Leadership becomes less about explaining the path and more about walking it. This is the part where choices matter, where your own relationship to risk shapes the systems you lead. Strategies stall when the people responsible for action hesitate, protect, or retreat. Fear delays decisions. It silences conversations. It hides behind analysis and rationalizations that keep us from the real action that leadership requires.

The Face, Frame, Forward model is no longer just a linear path. It becomes a daily rhythm. A cycle of noticing, naming, and moving over and over again. We'll explore how leaders bring this rhythm to life through trust-building behaviors, especially when fear is loud, stakes are high, and clarity is fogged by doubt.

We'll revisit the Can, Care, Do model of *Trust in Action* as a map to navigate through fear. When teams stall or fracture, it's rarely due to incompetence. More often, it's an unspoken breach of trust, usually triggered by fear.

We'll also explore fear—not as a weakness, but as a signal, a teacher, and a mirror. The problem is never fear itself. The problem is refusing to name it.

That's why Risk in Action is not a leadership destination. It's a rhythm of lived practice we return to, again and again, each time with more clarity and more courage to act. It's also why personal growth and enterprise performance are not separate conversations. They never were.

What lies ahead is a new question that only reveals itself when we choose to move. The old proverb says: "See no evil. Hear no evil. Speak no evil." In the world of risk, that's exactly the problem. We don't see what's in front of us. We don't hear what's trying to reach us. We freeze when it's time to speak up.

So here's the reframe:

See becomes the call of facing risk with clarity and courage.

Hear becomes the art of trust, listening through noise, discerning what's true.

Speak becomes the act of being fearFULL, saying that which scares us.

Risk doesn't ask us to close our eyes, cover our ears, or shut our mouths. It asks us to open them and walk in. This is where Risk in Action becomes real. In daily choices. In team dynamics. In what gets said and what gets silenced.

We'll close by turning our attention to what is emerging, to what is unfinished, and to a simple and daunting reality that the future is calling. The invitation is to think differently about risk and to live and lead in a way that transforms it. In the end, putting risk in action is the most human thing we can do.

7

To Act *or* Not to Act

"You can only see as far as your headlights, but
you can make the whole trip that way."

—E.L. Doctorow

At some point, every leader arrives at a juncture where the next step isn't certain, but standing still no longer feels safe. This is the turning point, the moment of choice.

I believe it must be a moment of action.

Action is about turning intention into motion. When leaders understand that risk, trust, and fear compete for their attention, they see action differently. How they engage with each force becomes a daily practice of moving forward. In that movement, risk shifts from uncertainty to clarity, trust moves from concept to lived experience, and fear becomes a lens that sharpens our focus.

Action is the cornerstone of progress and innovation. Without it, even the most carefully framed risks or the most profound trust remain intentions. Action carries us from the Land of Now to the Land of Next. It is the only place where ideas take form, where clarity is tested, and where growth becomes possible. Every model we've explored— facing reality, framing meaning, building trust to move forward—ultimately leads here, because action is where risk, trust, and fear all come alive together.

But what does action look like in a complex business environment? How does risk overlap and integrate with concepts like trust and fear? What else is at play on the levels of self, team, and system?

Action, Intention, and Motion

Action is the thread that connects everything. Risk demands it. Trust is built through it. And fear is only transformed by moving through it. .

In my risk model, the action is Forward. It's the choice to move even when clarity isn't complete. Forward breaks the cycle of oscillation and begins the journey into what's next.

In my trust model, the action is Do because trust lives in consistency. It's earned not by what you say, but by what you follow through on.

In the fear model, the action is fearFULL. It is not about

being fearless. It is about becoming familiar with fear, seeing it clearly, and choosing to move anyway. Fear is often a misread signal. When we fully engage with it, we see that much of what we feared was never real.

Each of these actions is different. Each emerges from a different context, yet each leads to the same destination and all share something vital: They must be chosen, lived, and practiced.

Now, in this final section, we turn to practice rooted in a simple philosophy: action. This chapter focuses on what it takes to move forward, not with certainty, but with clarity. It is about leading with trust, working with fear, and aligning risk with purpose. Reframing risk is not enough; at some point, we must walk the path. Trust is what allows us to take that walk, even through the fog of fear, when the outcome remains uncertain.

Taking Action Anyway

Leaders often hesitate, not because they don't care, but because decision fatigue has set in.

Endless debate wears down energy and morale. Clarity reduces this fatigue by focusing attention where it matters most. It helps leaders shift from debating symptoms to addressing root causes.

Inaction is still a choice. If we're going to lead through uncertainty, we can't wait for perfect conditions. We have to move. We must step forward with presence, act with intention, and trust that clarity often follows commitment.

I've watched teams circle the same decision week after week, not because they lacked data, but because they hadn't named what mattered most. Once they did, decisions that felt impossible suddenly became obvious.

But at some point, we must walk the path. We must take action in what I call the Action Universe: the space where leaders must recognize that risk, trust, and fear compete for their attention. In that moment, we begin to see action in a new light.

We must move Forward even when the outcome isn't guaranteed.

We must Do because trust lives in follow-through.

And we must be fearFULL, carrying our fear with clarity and courage.

Clarity in Motion

Clarity doesn't require perfection. It requires conviction. And conviction is built by knowing what matters most right now.

One biotech company I worked with illustrates this well. The organization is filled with brilliant people. Most had been wildly successful at other companies and knew how to get to the Land of Next. As the company began to mature, and as their research advanced from one stage to the next, something shifted. Despite all their experience, this was unfamiliar ground. The evolution of the business and the science required a different skill set than many of them had developed or applied.

What made this even more complex was that what the company was trying to do—how they were trying to design and deliver—had never really been done in this way. This wasn't just new to them; it was new, period.

That uncertainty became a fog. Teams were stuck. Some

Action

Turning intention into motion

The model below illustrates the interplay of risk, trust, and fear that surrounds a leader's ability to act. Meaningful action requires holding all three in view, and it is in working with this tension that the Action Universe comes to life.

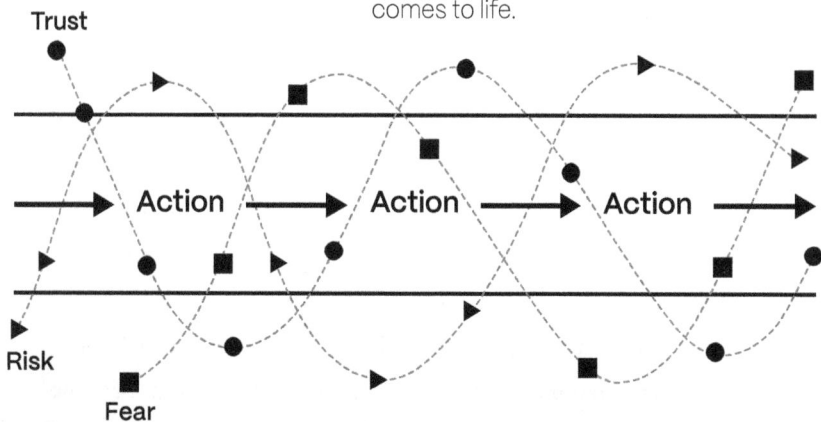

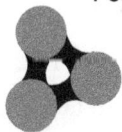

Trust

Creating the building blocks of action

When **Can, Care,** and **Do** come together, trust if formed, creating the connective tissue that makes action possible.

Risk

Creating clarity for action

When leaders use the **Face, Frame, Forward** method, risk shifts from being an obstacle in the way to becoming the way forward.

Fear

Finding freedom beyond the box

When leaders become **fearFULL,** they choose to sit with fear, take action, and move with clarity rather than pretending to be fearless.

masked it with confidence. Others froze. One leader who rec-ognized what was happening asked me for help. I worked with them to design an intervention centered on trust, a way to help the team find a common language and see that while they hadn't done this exact thing before, they had the skill, experience, and insight to take the step.

The shift came when they realized there was no roadmap. That also meant there were no wrong turns, just experiments.

This choice, by the leadership and by the team as a whole, is a great example of how moving even in the midst of incomplete data is about informed conviction. I've seen leaders at global companies reframe big operational shifts this way: Instead of asking, "Is this the perfect move?" they ask, "Is this the right next step given what we know now?" That framing reduces hesitation and increases shared ownership of decisions.

In this example, governance had to be redefined. Medical, clinical, and regulatory teams all had to move, support one another, and accept that some of what they tried would fail. The team came to realize this wasn't a flaw in the company, or in themselves. It was an inextricable part of what it means to take action. Failure wouldn't be a sign of weakness; it would be a sig-nal that they were innovating.

The workshop ended with three commitments:

- Create a no-blame, no-shame culture where failure was part of forward movement.

- Use a shared language of trust, grounded in the Can, Care, Do model (from my previous book, *Trust in Action*).

- Own the alignment between intent and impact, especially when the stakes are high.

Another key learning for the team was that clarity required something deeper: managing the polarities of growth. These leaders could choose new strategies because they were consciously navigating paradoxes. They brought structure to a previously scrappy environment without losing its entrepreneurial spark. They evolved from being purely science-led to becoming science-led, patient-driven, and market-driven. At the heart of this tension was the realization that both rigor and flexibility were essential. The leadership team had to balance control and autonomy, speed and diligence, science-driven decision-making and commercial readiness. In doing so, they shifted from trying to solve a single problem to managing the polarities that define the company's growth.

The ability to recognize that both sides were essential became a turning point. Instead of seeing these as competing forces, they began treating them as complementary tools in their leadership toolkit.

Polarity thinking allowed the team to see that these tensions weren't failures of focus. And clarity—real clarity—meant being able to stand in the middle of those tensions and still move forward. Leaders began transforming not only themselves, but their company, and in doing so, may well transform their industry.

At the time of this writing, the final outcome is still unknown. What we do know is that the clarity they found came in the commitment of the leaders to move.

Signal, Don't Solve

Acting with clarity is a must to truly lead well. But clarity is not *all*-knowing. It is simply knowing where you refuse to compromise. One of the most important distinctions leaders must learn is the difference between clarity and certainty. Certainty is about knowing exactly what will happen. Clarity is about knowing why you're moving and what you're trying to achieve. This is the beginning of informed, intentional action. And in a way, understanding this is the beginning of the rest of your life as a leader. Clarity is about knowing what matters enough that you won't compromise.

Sometimes the only thing you can compromise is your need for more time. Teams often get caught in circular reasoning, waiting for certainty, running decisions through endless committees. But clarity cuts through that. It says: This decision may not be perfect, but it's aligned with our purpose, and we must move.

We saw this vividly with AI. In 2023, OpenAI's launch of ChatGPT-4 triggered a global race. Companies scrambled to respond. The public called for guardrails. But the tech was already out in the world, being used, tested, scaled. The laws couldn't keep up. Yet even without perfect regulations or risk frameworks, organizations still had to act.[1,2]

In one team strategy meeting early in my consulting career, I saw this dynamic up close. The company was struggling to

---

1 "GPT-4," OpenAI, March 2023, https://openai.com/index/gpt-4-research/.

2 Krystal Hu, "ChatGPT Sets Record for Fastest-Growing User Base—Analyst Note," Reuters, February 1, 2023, https://www.reuters.com/technology/chatgpt-sets-record-fastest-growing-user-base-analyst-note-2023-02-01/.

shift from ESG reporting to trust reporting. They wanted a report that felt safe and conventional. Although I could clearly see the next step, they couldn't. Several executives thought the solution was another meeting or more data. In reality, the solution was simpler. I drafted the first version for them, putting words to the approach in a way that reflected their own language and actions. Once they saw the draft, the fear started to lift. They stopped debating whether to move and started focusing on *how* to move. Clarity, not certainty, became the compass. The commitment to move forward, even amid fog, became the only responsible choice.

Leading in the Mist

When we have the clarity of what matters most, we must help others see what's worth choosing. As leaders, we don't simply step into the unknown for ourselves. We step forward so we can return. Because real clarity, especially the kind that moves an organization, comes from walking others through the fog, not just pointing at the horizon from afar.

There is a place beyond fear, just past the fog, called the Land of Next. Every great leader must go there first, crossing alone through the haze of uncertainty. We do this not to escape or to become complacent and wait for others, but to see, to listen, and to understand what is truly real. To remember why others must want to be there. Reaching the Land of Next is just the beginning. Remember, the team is still in the fog, scattered across uncertain terrain. Some are only now waking to the shift, while others still cling to the comfort of the Land of Now. Heck, many may still be fondly remembering the Land of Was, and they're still two steps behind the risk line. They don't see it as the invitation it is; they see it as a barrier. So as leaders, we must return. Not in status, judgment, or with the need to prove we are ahead. We go back in the spirit of conveying what the Land of Next offers.

This isn't easy. We won't return to a parade or an entire group ready to go. So we must find the early adopters, the ones who feel both uneasy and excited about the change. The ones who sense that something is coming, that change is certain, but remain unsure of the next step. We must meet them where they are, not where they "should" be. We walk with them, building trust one step and one truth at a time.

Early adopters are rarely the loudest voices in the room. They're the ones quietly leaning in, asking thoughtful questions, sensing the shift before others do. As leaders, our job is to find these early movers and walk with them first. Then, as the momentum builds, others follow, because they trust the path being built.

This reminds me of the first follower theory, made popular by Derek Sivers in a short TED talk. In it, he narrates a video of a lone dancer starting to move in a public park. At first, people watch, amused or uncertain. But then one person joins in—not a leader, just someone willing to move. That *first follower* transforms the scene. Suddenly, the leader is no longer alone. And once there are two, a third joins, then a fourth. What once looked odd now looks brave and not risky. It now feels safe enough to try.

The insight is simple: Leadership is about creating the

conditions for someone else to feel safe stepping in second. I've come to learn that deep change doesn't come from brute force. When we acknowledge the courage of the first follower, the story shifts from individual leadership to shared momentum, sparking a revolution of change through invitation.

Change rarely happens as a mass migration. It unfolds as a movement of moments. When trust becomes the bridge and care becomes the guide, the first steps become the way. Others follow not because they were told to, but because they were met.

Risk comes to life through steps taken together. The Land of Next is built through aligned strategy and a shared story. Leadership's invisible labor is practicing care as conviction, helping others step into uncertainty even after you've already crossed. Care is what binds us, and clarity is what moves us.

Crossing the Line

Crossing the line is about rejecting an outdated philosophy of risk. For too long, risk management meant compliance. It meant standing two steps behind the line to avoid what was unfamiliar, unpredictable, or uncomfortable. Leaders were taught that risk was something to manage from a distance, something to mitigate or control and not something to engage with directly. Sometimes that caution was right. There are lines we shouldn't cross. Moments when risk signals real harm, where hesitation protects what matters most.

Many of the lines drawn in today's organizations are rooted in fear yet masked as certainty. They're relics from a time when standing still felt like the safest choice. As we rethink risk in today's world, leadership requires a different stance. The line we're called to cross is the one that separates outdated control-based thinking from purpose-driven action. It's the line that turns risk from an obstacle into the way forward. The important lesson is knowing which lines hold us back and which ones hold us up. Some keep us trapped in cycles of delay, indecision, and self-preservation, while others are drawn by assumptions that no longer make sense, and perhaps never did.

I watched this play out with one executive who had been pushing hard to drive strategic change. She had spent months moving her leadership team through the transition, helping them build the clarity needed to act with confidence. But as the next phase approached, she hit a new roadblock: Her board wasn't moving. They were still stuck debating assumptions she had long since tested and resolved. Her instinct was frustration. She had already done this work. Why should she have to go back?

This question unlocked the mystery for both of us. Leadership is never about leading from the front. Frequently, a leader must go back, intentionally, to help others get to the Land of Next.

She returned to the Land of Now out of confidence, not because she doubted her path. She realized her job wasn't just to lead forward. She had a responsibility to reach back and bring others with her. That's what crossing the line really means. Getting to the Land of Next is not a solo achievement. It's a commitment to become the guide others will need when their own clarity runs thin.

Control the Controllables

In traditional risk management, we talk about "controls," the mechanisms we put in place to prevent bad things from happening: policies, approvals, escalation procedures, mandatory training, communication rollouts, and change management strategies. Most organizations rely on these to demonstrate defensibility, especially when things go wrong. They say, "We had the policy. The individual didn't follow it." That narrative might once have satisfied regulators or enforcement agencies, but not anymore.

At AstraZeneca, I began to realize we had overdone it. Our Code of Conduct had ballooned to thirty pages. The supporting policies added up to more than a thousand additional pages, layer upon layer of expectations an employee was supposed to read, remember, and comply with. My team and I came to learn that compliance without comprehension is just noise.

One pivotal moment came during a global compliance meeting. We reviewed the overwhelming volume of documentation and realized that employees were unclear of the expectations and had become disengaged because they were overwhelmed. The more we added, the less they read. I remember one employee saying: "I want to do the right thing when it comes to meal limits, but I have no idea what that is anymore. We have a meal limit for on-site, off-site, doctor, nurse, staff, and sometimes it changes by state." That comment stuck with me. This was a clear failure of design I had to own.

We started asking different questions. What if the control isn't the policy but the moment of choice? What if we embedded accountability into the process, not just the paperwork?

So we did. One example: Rather than stating a meal limit in a policy and hoping employees remembered it during a client dinner, we programmed the limit directly into the expense reporting system. If someone exceeded the threshold, the system flagged it, and their manager had to approve the exception.

But we didn't stop there. If that approval occurred and the issue persisted, we didn't investigate the employee who exceeded the limit; we investigated the manager who approved the exception and failed to address the behavior. The *decision* became the control, not the expense report.

Clarity also means building systems that reduce low-value decision making. One client realized they were burning hours every month debating expense approvals under $100. By setting clear thresholds and automating small decisions, they freed leadership time for higher-risk, higher-impact calls. Small operational shifts like this create space for real leadership.

This is what it means to control the controllables: building accountability into the moment of action. Embedding risk awareness into the speed and point of business. It's a shift from asking employees to memorize rules to designing systems that reflect values. It's about driving accountability by placing it where it belongs.

Purpose-Aligned Risk-Taking

Not all risks are created equal. The risks worth taking are the ones that align with your deeper purpose, those that move you closer to the leader, team, or organization you're meant to become.

I learned this when I decided to transform AstraZeneca's

environmental program from a reduction model to a removal model. The safe choice would have been to celebrate what we'd already accomplished and make incremental improvements.

But I could see that this approach wasn't enough. The climate crisis demanded transformation, not just optimization. So I chose to risk the team's confidence in my leadership, risk the perception that I was asking too much, and risk the possibility of failure. The alternative was complicity in a system that was already failing.

The risk aligned with my purpose. And that alignment gave me the courage to act. This wasn't an isolated leadership choice. I've worked with organizations standing at similar crossroads where doing what was expected felt safe, but doing what was needed felt right. In several cases, leaders chose to move forward because it was values-aligned. Whether it was advancing access to care, accelerating sustainability efforts, or speaking out when silence felt easier, their actions were driven by purpose. The lesson is clear: When risk and purpose align, action becomes the only real choice.

Invitation to Innovation

Innovation is what comes next. It's the new idea that hasn't been done before, the one that sits just across the gap, waiting. That's why I created this metaphor: Risk is the gap, trust is the bridge, and fear is the fog. When I examine risk, I see how trust and fear pull leaders and organizations in opposite directions. I can't write about risk without also writing about trust. And I can't write about trust without addressing fear. The three are inseparable.

They shape our daily decisions. They influence our actions. And when we learn to see risk clearly, we begin to understand how trust and fear combine to create the conditions for breakthrough thinking and meaningful change.

At its core, innovation happens when we face reality honestly, acknowledging both opportunities and challenges. It happens when we frame what matters most, connecting risk to purpose and values. It moves forward when we take action aligned with our mission. And it sustains when we build trust systematically, creating the psychological safety needed for bold moves, and when we work with fear constructively, seeing it as a signal for what matters most.

When these elements come together, we develop fearFULL leadership, which gives us the ability to act boldly and precisely because we understand what's at stake.

This idea sets the stage for the Action Universe. Leaders need the tools to address risk, trust and fear if we hope to continue to move forward. In Chapter 8, "Trust in Action," we'll explore how to operationalize trust as a leadership trait and as a living system. In Chapter 9, "Fill 'Er Up," we'll explore fearFULL leadership: the kind it takes to keep moving when you think everything around you signals retreat.

8

Trust: Can, Care, Do

"The best way to find out if you can trust
somebody is to trust them."

—Ernest Hemingway

How Can, Care, Do Stops the Oscillation

I n my previous book *Trust in Action*, I introduced the Can, Care, Do model of trust. What I've learned since then is how directly this model addresses the oscillation that keeps leaders, teams, and even entire systems from moving forward. When people get stuck, debating without deciding, planning without executing, it's rarely due to a lack of intellect or even effort. It's a breakdown of trust. The breakdown can usually be traced to a gap in one of three areas: capability (**Can**), connection (**Care**), or commitment (**Do**).

We know from neuroscience that trust and fear are closely linked in the brain. They compete for the same mental real estate. When one rises, the other tends to fall. When leaders oscillate, it often activates the amygdala, the brain's threat detection center, causing teams to perceive ambiguity as danger. This biological response triggers hesitation, hyper-analysis, or retreat. Applying Can, Care, Do can interrupt this neurobiological spiral, signaling safety and encouraging action. By recognizing and repairing breakdowns in trust, leaders send a powerful message: "You're safe to move."

To understand how trust unlocks action, we need to break down each element more deeply and explore how they help us cross the gap from the Land of Now to the Land of Next. This takes us from theory to application of real stories, real systems, and real shifts. Trust is the bridge we must navigate between where we are and where we aspire to be, without fear, without hesitation, and with clarity of direction. This transforms the unknown from a vast valley into a bridge. And Can, Care, Do is how we build that bridge, one step at a time.

Can: The Trust of Capability

Can is about the confidence that something, or someone, is able. It's confidence in skills, knowledge, preparation, and self-belief. It's about being enough instead of being the ideal.

In teams, a lack of Can shows up as second-guessing, excessive oversight, or quiet withholding. Leaders might say, "I trust you," but their actions of hovering, editing, or avoiding delegation clearly signal doubt. Internally, individuals may hesitate

Trust: Creating the building blocks of action

When **Can, Care,** and **Do** come together, something interesting happens. Trust is formed. Trust is the connective tissue that makes positive action possible. It creates the building blocks for a successful self, team, and system.

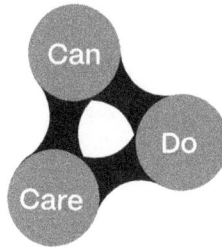

Self

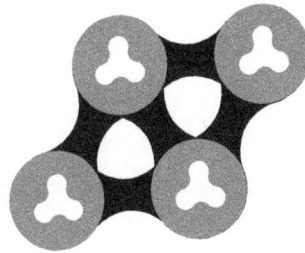

Team

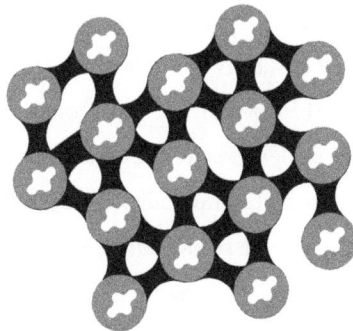

System

to speak up or take initiative because they question their own readiness.

The neuroscience of capability also shows up here. Teams operating in low-Can environments often experience cognitive overload. They burn energy second-guessing tasks, fearing blame for mistakes, or overchecking their work. Over time, this creates decision fatigue and reduces overall organizational velocity.

I've seen how Can shows up in my own life, especially when self-trust feels uncertain. When I accepted leadership of the Environmental, Health, and Safety team, I knew I wasn't fully technically trained for the environmental side of the work. But I trusted my ability to learn. I deepened my expertise so I could challenge and evolve our GHG program from reduction to removal. That was a transformation of Can in myself, and eventually in the team and system. Within a year, our environmental team transitioned from being compliance-oriented to innovation-driven. They led one of the first net-zero strategies in the industry.

This was frustrating for my team. As subject matter experts, they were used to having another SME lead them. But as things changed, the organization was looking for experts to be led by general leaders who could challenge and change their perception. So though the team was frustrated at first, and I had to develop my Can, I also had to leverage Care. In the end, the team developed a groundbreaking strategy that allowed them to fully embrace their purposes. Their capabilities allowed them to transform themselves, AstraZeneca, and the world through creating the new standard that all companies would follow in the future.

One story that stands out comes from a pharmaceutical team preparing for a high-stakes product launch. The team had technical expertise, but because leadership hadn't clearly framed decision rights, individuals hesitated to act. When we mapped the Can, Care, Do gaps, it became clear: The missing piece was permission to act with autonomy. By clarifying Can expectations and giving teams room to execute, velocity increased almost overnight.

Can is also about self-trust. When I was asked to lead the Environmental, Health and Safety team, I was morbidly obese and felt deeply conflicted about being the face of a health team. I knew I would have both professional and personal challenges with the new role. That moment revealed how every risk we face at work touches something deeper: our sense of worth, our need for control, our fear of being exposed. Eventually, I worked with a nutritionist, lost over ninety pounds, and used that transformation to show the team that change was possible. That experience reminded me that Can isn't about mastery; it's about motion.

Building Can means investing in learning and feedback. It requires naming what's expected and offering the support to get there. High Can environments are development-rich because they are not mistake-free. People act because they trust they'll learn through the doing.

Care: The Trust of Intent and Connection

Care is the belief that others have your back and that you have theirs. It's about shared purpose, aligned values, and the courage to be vulnerable. Without Care, capability can feel transactional. With Care, it becomes relational.

Neuroscience research highlights that Care, at its core, is about social safety. When people feel cared for, oxytocin levels rise, opening up cognitive pathways for collaboration and innovation.

The shift from shareholder primacy to stakeholder capitalism revealed how Care functions as a leadership signal rooted in values, not sentiment. One of the most memorable moments came from Dame Polly Courtice, a longtime board advisor and ethics leader. After reviewing our revised trust strategy, she pulled me aside and said, "You didn't just change the slide deck—you changed the room." We had moved from checking boxes to opening dialogue. From defensiveness to listening. Her feedback reminded me that when leaders genuinely act from a place of care, people feel it. And they respond, intellectually *and* emotionally.

I learned the importance of Care when I inadvertently excluded a friend from a conversation. She was a woman, an educator, and I had focused only on men when asking about career satisfaction. Realizing my blind spot, I apologized publicly and sincerely. That moment became a lasting reminder: Care must be shown, not just stated.

Care also means challenging assumptions. During a major corporate presentation, I asked why our target for women in executive leadership was only 33 percent. We had 51 percent women in the company. Why were we celebrating less-than-fair? That challenge, rooted in Care, led to a revised goal of 50 percent and to decisive action. Over the next three years, we transformed our leadership and were at 48.1 percent, years ahead of the original goal.

Restoring Care means practicing presence, listening generously, and surfacing conflict before it erodes trust and shows up as silence or resentment. It means choosing curiosity over certainty. One of the most relevant recent examples comes from a 2025 *Harvard Business Review* article by Ron Carucci. He described how a chief executive, facing stakeholder skepticism and internal tension, launched weekly "stakeholder walkthroughs." These weren't the typical polished town halls. The meetings were open sessions where board members, frontline staff, and community advocates voiced concerns and offered suggestions. Within months, internal and external trust scores improved by over 20 percent. The walk-throughs showed consistent care and people felt seen, heard, and included in the process.[1]

When Care is present, people show up for each other, not just the job. They take risks because they believe they'll be supported for trying, not punished for failing.

---

1 Ron Carucci, "Executive Teams Are Losing Stakeholders' Confidence. Here's How to Get It Back," Harvard Business Review, April 2025, https://hbr.org/2025/04 /executive-teams-are-losing-stakeholders-confidence-heres-how-to-get-it-back.

Do: The Trust of Commitment

Do is the trust of follow-through. It's about taking action and doing what you say you will do. It's how trust moves from concept to reality. You can have all the capability and care in the world, but without commitment, trust won't exist.

In organizations, a lack of Do looks like the endless strategy loop, brilliant plans, no execution. People talk about priorities, but calendars tell another story. Meetings end with "we'll revisit this next time." The system turns its leaders into experts at delay.

Nothing breaks trust faster than bold promises with no follow-through. I saw this firsthand at a healthcare company where repeated change announcements led to little real action. Employees became cynical. They bought into the various strategies that always sounded great at first. The problem was that promises never turned into delivery. Trust was lost because visible patterns of inaction.

Leaders repaired that Do gap by creating a visible commitment board, publicly tracking which strategic promises were in flight and which had been completed. Within six months, employee engagement rose significantly as people saw their leaders doing what they said they would do.

Another important Do practice is microcommitments. This is the leadership behavior of rebuilding trust through small, visible steps, not one giant overhaul. The decision to return a call on time, close a feedback loop, or deliver a promised update are all small actions that accumulate into a culture of Do.

Slack's early growth illustrates this lesson. After launching what began as an internal communication tool, the team quickly realized that progress depends more on momentum than mastery.

Despite having a sound strategy and a strong team, they refused to wait for perfect alignment. Instead, Slack's founders set a simple rule: ship fast, learn faster. Within thirty days, they released a minimum viable product and built their future around the feedback it generated. Every iteration sparked new energy, because users felt heard, teams re-engaged, and customer adoption accelerated. It was the choice to keep moving with clarity rather than wait for perfection that propelled them forward.[1]

We experienced this in our environmental shift as well. After launching our climate targets, I knew we needed more than aspirational language. So I pushed our team to go from "reduce" to "remove." That small change created tension, and it created action. Within months, we launched one of the first net-zero, science-based programs in the industry.

Do doesn't require certainty. It requires commitment. The most trusted leaders don't have all the answers. They're just the ones who go first.

Hold and Move

One of the hardest tensions in leadership is to care enough to wait, and to commit enough to act. This is the paradox of action. Trust doesn't mean rushing. Neither does it mean stalling until everything is known.

We hold two truths: Uncertainty is real, and so is responsibility. Leaders must feel deeply and act decisively. They must listen

---

1 "From 0 to $1B: Slack's Founder Shares Their Epic Launch Strategy," *First Round Review*, https://review.firstround.com/from-0-to-1b-slacks-founder-shares-their -epic-launch-strategy/.

fully and still make the call. The Can, Care, Do model reminds us that trust is active, not passive. It's built through practiced discernment: knowing when to pause and when to move.

This paradox is both emotional and operational. I've worked with organizations trapped in pilot mode, afraid to scale decisions until every variable is perfect. The Can, Care, Do lens helps leaders navigate this by asking themselves whether they're holding because they care or because they fear. Are they moving because they're ready or because they're tired of waiting? Trust comes from making these distinctions explicit.

One practice that reduces organizational anxiety and reinforces trust during moments of movement is decision transparency, narrating why you're acting now. Saying out loud, "We know this isn't perfect, but we have enough to act," signals both Care and Do.

I once worked with a global leadership team struggling to launch a new compliance initiative. The data wasn't complete, and key stakeholders still had unanswered questions. But the CEO stood up in a leadership town hall and said, "We've framed this as much as we can. The risk of delay now outweighs the risk of imperfection. We're moving." That single statement unlocked momentum. More importantly, it became a leadership signal to the broader organization: Inaction has a cost.

Stopping the Oscillation

When trust breaks, teams oscillate. They cycle between Can and Care, afraid to Do. Or they over-rely on Do, skipping over Care and eroding Can. Real action comes when all three work in harmony. When I trust your skill, your intent, and your commitment, I follow. When I trust my own, I lead.

In my work with executive teams, I began noticing a pattern: When leaders consistently showed up with clarity, care, and follow-through, something shifted. Trust didn't just improve; it accelerated. That insight led me to the trust *flywheel*, a concept I first heard from Joseph Myers. It describes how momentum builds when small trust-building behaviors stack over time. The Can, Care, Do model feeds that flywheel. Each time a leader closes a trust gap, the system gains energy. Teams start making decisions faster. Feedback becomes more direct, and ownership spreads.

I've seen the Can, Care, Do model reduce oscillation not just at the team level, but across entire organizations. One *Fortune* 100 client used the model as a diagnostic lens during a post-merger integration. They mapped trust gaps across business units, highlighting where capability needed to be reinforced, where cross-functional Care was missing, and where execution bottlenecks reflected a lack of Do. That exercise became the foundation for their next-year leadership priorities.

And it's not just systems. Individuals oscillate too. In coaching sessions, I've seen senior leaders stuck in the "high-Can, low-Do trap." They overanalyze. They review data endlessly. They over-research because their self-identity is tied to expertise, but they struggle to act.

The idea of "re-trusting" is especially important when teams are caught in oscillation. That hesitation often stems not just from the current gap, but from unresolved history. Teams stall because prior failures haven't been addressed. Naming this openly—for example, saying, "We're hesitating because the last rollout failed"—can be the first step toward reestablishing Do and moving forward. Restoring momentum starts with locating the gap, naming it, and then taking one action to close it. Then another. And another.

When we stop the oscillation, we break the cycle of doubt and delay. We give ourselves, and those we lead, permission to move forward even when things are uncertain. When trust becomes actionable, it generates momentum and shifts stagnation into movement, ambiguity into shared direction, and fear into fuel for progress. Yet fear never disappears; it hides in the shadows, shaping choices we pretend are rational. Leaders who deny it become prisoners of it. The only way forward is to sit down with fear, face it up close, and strip it of its disguise. Not to conquer it, but to recognize it and to become fearFULL, seeing fear clearly and choosing to move anyway. To move forward, we must do more than acknowledge fear, we must sit with it until it tells us the truth. That is where we turn next: into the terrain of fear itself, and the work of learning how to sit with it intimately, until what once held us back begins to show us the way forward.

9

Fill 'Er Up

"Leadership has never been this personal."

—Amon Wolfe, 432 Hz

Speak the Unspeakable

Fear is familiar yet often ignored. It shows up everywhere from boardrooms to our kitchen conversations, and we rarely name it. We act around it, explain past it, and make decisions shaped by it, all without saying the word. Fear is in big decisions and quiet doubts, and yet we rarely talk about it, at least not honestly. Instead, we project confidence. We talk about courage and grit, and we try to hide fear. We dismiss fear as one of those childhood illusions—like a monster under the bed or shadows on the wall—and pretend we've long since outgrown it. We are leaders. There's no way we could ever have fear. We are fearless.

The truth, though, is that fear never really leaves. It just waits to show up during a moment of change, challenge, or when we have to face the truth. When it shows up, we get to make a choice: Shrink back or fill up.

In fact, fear is both psychological and physiological. Based on the Lead Beyond Fear model created by 432 Hz—a leadership development organization named after the frequency often associated with harmony and resonance—when fear becomes chronic or unrecognized, it triggers biological stress. Metrics like heart rate variability (HRV), cortisol levels, and breath rate all shift when we're operating from fear, even if we're not consciously aware of it. Leadership capacity is about mindset and nervous system readiness. Once again, this is about building awareness, practicing consistently, and developing the leadership reflex to respond with clarity and intention.

And that's what caught me off guard. While I thought I was managing my fear, my body was telling a different story. The shallow breathing before a tough conversation. The restless nights before a high-stakes decision. The racing heart in meetings where something important needed to be said but wasn't.

I learned to normalize it, calling it stress or executive pressure. Just another demanding, busy week, I told myself. But ultimately, underneath it all, lived my fear.

Fear that I'd make the wrong call or that I'd disappoint people I care about. Fear that speaking up would create conflict I wasn't ready to handle, or that if I slowed down, everything would fall apart. What no one ever told me is that fear doesn't always feel like panic. Sometimes it disguises itself as over-thinking, or shows up as procrastination, or hides in the quiet moments when you play small, even when that voice inside you says you're meant to go bigger. It shows up in the pauses between decisions and in the sideways glances around a conference table. In the stories we tell ourselves to stay comfortable. Fear's job is to keep us still.

This is the tension we face as leaders. Fear is real, and yet we're still called to move. The organizations we run and the people we lead want progress to drive innovation, and they wanted it yesterday. Growth targets, transformation plans, bold revenue projections all come with a sense of urgency that leaves little room for doubt. And yet here we are, standing in leadership, staring down decisions with no guaranteed path. Just because someone says the organization will double its revenue in five or ten years doesn't make it true. There's no certainty, no map with clear markers, and all we feel is pressure.

In the back of our minds, we're confident the organization will survive. But what about us? What about the people around us? What happens when we keep pushing without pause? When we trade clarity for speed? When we pretend we're fine, even as our breath shortens and our patience thins?

We tell ourselves we just need a break. We can refresh over a long weekend, mini vacation, or just by taking some time to recharge. What I'm bringing up, however, goes deeper than rest. I'm not talking about personal time off (PTO) or quick getaways. This is about *stopping*. Seriously, truly stopping long enough to regroup and to ask ourselves, and each other, the harder question: What's the first step we need to take when tensions are high and none of us feels brave enough to say, "I don't know"?

At times, courage shows up less in charging forward and more in admitting we're human. One of my favorite mentors once said, "Humans are the only things that, when we hit pause, we begin." It is only when we stop that we create the pace to think, imagine, get out of the here and now, and dream again. Pausing isn't quitting. It's the moment we reconnect with what matters most, so we can move forward with greater clarity and intention.

Failures of Fearlessness

What's the opposite of fearless? Fearful. For most of my life, that word carried a negative weight and felt like weakness, hesitation, the absence of action. I believe deeply in action. So much so that both of my books have " . . . *in Action*" in their titles. Action, when it's informed and intentional, is what drives innovation and change.

Throughout my leadership career, I believed my job was to be fearless. To push forward without hesitation. To show confidence at all costs. That's what leadership required, right? Unshakable certainty, boldness, and complete control of the outcomes. That worked until it didn't. Things started to change right around my first conversation with Amon Wolfe, founder of Fearless in Thought, who helped shift that belief.

I realized I had placed the wrong emphasis on the wrong syllable. Literally and metaphorically.

The goal was never to be "fear-less." The goal needed to be fearFULL: to face the fear, frame it in my context, examine what I was feeling, and ask, "What am I so afraid of?"

In doing that, something unexpected happened. I saw that most of my fear wasn't even real. It was a story or a construct I had inherited from those around me, not something I had chosen. The fear wasn't my enemy. My avoidance of fear was the culprit. We don't build trust by eliminating fear. We build trust by moving through it, fully aware, fully awake, and fully human.

When we fail to acknowledge our fears, they don't disappear. They just go underground. They start influencing our decisions in ways we don't recognize or understand. The leaders who inspire the most trust are the ones who acknowledge fear, examine it, and then consciously choose how to respond.

My job *was* to fear nothing. Now I know it is to examine why I fear something, to sit with that fear, and still choose to act. To show up, to try, to fail, and to trust that everything in between is part of the process. That's what FearFULL leadership looks like.

All in the Family

We often talk about fear and trust as opposites, as if one cancels out the other. But they're actually more like family. They live together and show up in the same conversations. And more often than not, they fight for the same thing: our attention when risk is present.

Trust and fear don't take turns. At any moment, both are present to nudge and shape how we interpret risk and whether

we move. Fear makes risk feel bigger. Trust makes risk feel possible. The leader's job isn't to banish fear or blindly follow trust;
it's to recognize the dynamic and choose with clarity.

Trust and fear constantly compete for risk's attention. One
says, "You've got this." The other whispers, "What if you don't?"
One invites movement. The other builds caution. And in every
high-stakes moment, we get to decide which one we will follow.

Fear is a force that influences every part of the trust system.
It convinces us we're not capable. It distorts our intent. It makes
follow-through feel risky or even impossible. But fear doesn't
stop at trust. It also affects how we engage with risk itself, how
we face the unknown, frame what matters, and move forward
into the new.

It is important to revisit the Can, Care, Do model through
the lens of fear, and layer in how fear also plays out in the Face,
Frame, Forward model of risk. Because fear doesn't just live
inside us. It shapes the systems we lead. When we name our
fear, sit with it, and choose to act anyway, we begin to practice a
different kind of leadership, one that doesn't wait for certainty,
but moves with clarity. That kind of leadership has a name: fear-
FULL leadership.

FearFULL leadership shows up when leaders confront
fear not by pushing it away, but by working with it. In the
case studies that follow, we'll revisit the Can, Care, Do model
of trust and see how fear influences each case. We will also
begin to notice how fear shapes risk itself by how we face the
unknown, frame what matters, and move forward. These case
studies are reminders of what it means to lead with clarity in
the presence of fear.

Can: The Trust of Capability
Risk Lens: Facing the Unknown
Case Study: Satya Nadella and Fear of Inadequacy

When Satya Nadella became CEO of Microsoft in 2014, he faced intense impostor syndrome. Surrounded by tech icons, he feared he wasn't up to the task. But instead of hiding that fear, he faced it and led anyway. Nadella leaned into learning and vulnerability, shifting Microsoft's culture from "know-it-all" to "learn-it-all." He didn't try to erase the fear. He reframed it. And in doing so, he helped the organization reframe risk from a threat to a growth opportunity.[1]

Lesson: Fear of inadequacy can be a doorway, not a dead end. Facing it with humility and trust unlocks capability and changes culture.

Care: The Trust of Intent and Alignment
Risk Lens: Framing What Matters
Case Study: CVS Health and the Tobacco Decision

In 2014, CVS Health chose to stop selling tobacco products across 7,600 US stores—knowing it would cost them an estimated $2 billion in annual revenue. The fear of short-term financial backlash was real. But leadership reframed the risk:

---

1 "Microsoft Board Names Satya Nadella as CEO," Microsoft, February 4, 2014, https://news.microsoft.com/source/2014/02/04/microsoft-board-names-satya -nadella-as-ceo/.

Continuing to sell tobacco was a greater threat to their identity as a healthcare company. By aligning their business model with their purpose, CVS sent a clear signal that its brand reflects values in action.[1,2]

Lesson: Fear often tempts leaders to protect the status quo. Real care reframes risk around long-term integrity and moves with purpose, even when the cost is high.

Do: The Trust of Commitment and Follow-through
Risk Lens: Moving Forward
Case Study: FKA Haeckels and Radical Transparency

In 2024, FKA Haeckels, a UK-based skincare brand, rebranded to distance itself from the legacy of Ernst Haeckel and his ties to scientific racism. They could have made the change quietly. Instead, they acted openly, explaining the decision, engaging customers, and publishing real-time sustainability data alongside it. The greater fear was staying silent, and by moving

1 Phil Wahba and Julie Steenhuysen, "CVS Becomes First Big U.S. Drugstore Chain to Drop Tobacco," Reuters, February 5, 2014, https://www.reuters.com/article/lifestyle/cvs-becomes-first-big-us-drugstore-chain-to-drop-tobacco-idUSBREA140RR/.

2 "CVS Caremark to Stop Selling Tobacco at All CVS/pharmacy Locations," PR Newswire, February 5, 2014, https://www.prnewswire.com/news-releases/cvs-caremark-to-stop-selling-tobacco-at-all-cvspharmacy-locations-243662651.html.

forward transparently, they built deeper trust and stronger brand loyalty.[1, 2]

Lesson: Integrity requires movement. When fear urges silence, leaders who act with clarity signal courage and earn trust.

What these stories have in common is simple, yet hard to live. Trust and fear are always battling for our attention. While it may be easy to spot fear in hindsight, or in someone else's story, it's much harder to recognize in real time when it's happening inside of us. And it's even harder when risk is present, because fear distorts how we see ourselves and how we see the path forward.

That was the realization waiting for me at a FEAR Workshop, a curated gathering of US leaders exploring the role of fear and how to work through it. I've often been able to help my direct reports, peers, and those I work with name how fear showed up for them. I wasn't yet ready to name how it was showing up in me, at least not until someone pushed me to a place where I could finally stop circling and admit the truth about what I feared.

---

1 Dom Bridges, "Letter—People Care. Planet Care," FKA Haeckels, November 2024, https://www.haeckels.co.uk/pages/letter.

2 Nateisha Scott, "Why the Brand Formerly Known as Haeckels Is Relaunching," Vogue Business, November 2024, https://www.voguebusiness.com/story/beauty/why -the-brand-formerly-known-as-haeckels-is-relaunching.

What Do You Fear?

I've spent most of my career helping others navigate fear by coaching teams through uncertainty, guiding colleagues through tough decisions, and sitting with direct reports as they worked through doubt, hesitation, and self-imposed limits. Naming fear for others came naturally. But naming it for myself was something else entirely. That required a level of honesty I wasn't used to offering inward.

I told myself I was self-aware and that I understood how fear operated in leadership. However, understanding fear in theory is very different from experiencing it in real time, especially when the stakes feel personal and the story gets uncomfortably close.

It became clear to me the day I attended the FEAR Workshop hosted by Amon, whom I mentioned earlier. He gave us all full disclosure upfront, and we still agreed to jump right in. He asked us to sit in a circle and be fully present; then he would ask each of us a question. We all smiled and agreed, many of us meeting one another for the first time.

It wasn't until we stepped into that circle—eyes closed, slowing our breathing, and settling into stillness—that the weight of it landed when we all heard the question for the first time.

Amon said one of our names. Then he asked:

"What do you fear?"

And that's when I realized what I was about to experience. The question wasn't asking what I feared *in theory*. It wasn't about professional stress or even personal worries. It was deeper. It was truthfully asking: What is keeping you trapped in your Land of Now and preventing you from stepping into your Land of Next?

Amon turned to me:

"Jim . . . what do you fear?"

I gave an answer.

And just as with everyone else, he knew it wasn't my real answer.

So he simply asked me again:

"What do you fear?"

I kept answering with leadership-sounding responses.

Fear of getting it wrong.

Fear of not being effective enough.

Again, Amon wasn't satisfied—because he knew *I* wasn't.

He saw I was circling.

He asked me again:

"What do you fear?"

Finally, I said it:

"Self-chaos."

I realized I wasn't afraid of others. I was afraid of what their fear had taught me to believe about myself. That I wasn't worthy of peace. That my capacity to love others couldn't include me. What I feared wasn't about them. It was about me.

I had spent years offering love outward, while withholding it inward. Fear told me I wasn't worthy of rest, healing, wholeness, peace, love. It was only when I stopped letting others define the limits of love that I began to see myself clearly. The heart of my journey was being honest with myself, even when others expected authenticity on their terms. That's when the quiet battle inside me began to settle. For years, I thought I was moving forward when I was just circling larger and larger loops around my purpose, around my pain, around the very love I denied myself. Fear kept me orbiting what mattered most. I learned the hard way that circles don't move us forward. They contain us.

Only when I faced my fear—not pushed or explained it away, but truly faced it—did I step out of the circle. Forward wasn't a plan that evening. It was a breakthrough for me. It was my surrender. Coming out of that moment, something else became clear. For so much of my life, I had internalized other people's fears, their need for me to shrink, to stay small, to soften parts of myself to make others comfortable. Their fear didn't need to become my identity, and it should never have been my burden to carry.

In that summit, in that room, with those people, for the first time, I had nothing to fear. Not from them, not from the truth, and most importantly, not from myself. That was the first step. The moment I realized that fear, when left unnamed, had been driving more of my decisions than I cared to admit.

This is the foundation of the bigger pattern of how fear embeds itself into how we think. It shapes how we operate and how we experience risk. I wish I had a dime for every time I was told to manage risk by avoiding it, staying away from the line, keeping things safe, or minimizing exposure.

Underneath all that risk-avoidance was something more personal: someone's fear of the unknown, of failure, of stepping too far into the gap. That's why naming fear matters, despite all the self-help and corporate jargon we hear today about bringing your whole self to work, personal growth, authentic leadership, inclusive decision-making, informed risk-taking, and building trust. If we can't name the fear, we'll never see how it's shaping the risks we're too afraid to take.

Fear in Action

Fear doesn't announce itself in the boardroom. It doesn't show up with a label or a warning. It shows up in questions, hesitation, second-guessing. It hides behind strategy decks and executive polish. But make no mistake, fear is there, quietly shaping the choices leaders make and the risks they avoid. In executive boardrooms and coaching sessions, fear shows up in all kinds of disguises:

Fear of irrelevance: "Will my experience still matter as the world changes?"

Fear of abandonment: "If I make the wrong call, will I lose support?"

Fear of exposure: "What if I'm found out as unqualified or uncertain?"

Fear of expansion: "What if success consumes me?"

These aren't hypothetical questions. They're the internal soundtrack playing behind executive decisions every day. A 2024 Korn Ferry study found that 72% of senior leaders cited internal doubt, not market forces, as their greatest obstacle during strategic decision-making. This is fear in a tailored suit.

When fear stays unnamed, it drives overperformance or avoidance, causing us to work too hard or pull back entirely, anything to stay safe. So we overwork, overcontrol, or wait with the hope someone else will act first. In risk language, this is oscillation: swinging between extreme action and total inaction without conscious control. The organization lurches or freezes because leaders are making decisions from a place of fear-based distortion.

What makes this even more complex is how our physiology feeds our mindset. Chronic stress is a chemical and neurological state. When leaders operate with elevated cortisol levels or show reduced heart rate variability (HRV), both measurable through wearables and biometrics, they're more likely to fall into fear-driven behaviors. Stress physically narrows cognitive range, shrinking the brain's capacity for long-term thinking, creativity, and emotional regulation. We become reactive instead of reflective.

Though we maybe told this is a leadership weakness or even a personal flaw, the reality is that it's biology doing what it was designed to do: Prioritize survival over strategy. The challenge in leadership is that what looks like survival in the short term often creates long-term risk.

Fear distorts more than decision-making. It affects how leaders show up interpersonally. Some leaders become micromanagers, tightening control to reduce uncertainty. Others become people-pleasers, avoiding conflict to preserve harmony. Some shut down emotionally, withdrawing from relationships and making decisions in isolation. Others double down on perfectionism, hoping flawless execution will inoculate them from criticism. The behavior changes. The root cause remains the same. That's why naming the fear is essential. Until fear becomes visible, it remains in control.

This is an important discussion because fear isn't just about individual behavior. Fear becomes contagious in organizations. Teams start mirroring the leader's anxiety. Conversations grow guarded. Psychological safety erodes. Innovation slows because people are afraid of making the wrong move. Risk becomes something to avoid, rather than navigate.

In many organizations, the cultural cost of fear shows up in three patterns:

- **Overanalysis:** Teams collect data endlessly, stalling action under the guise of being thorough.
- **Blame culture:** Failures trigger defensiveness and finger-pointing instead of learning.
- **Silent meetings:** People nod along publicly, then privately resist or disengage.

Leaders don't wake up intending to create these environments. Fear does it for them. This is also where the opportunity sits. Because if fear can spread, so can courage. If fear can create distortion, awareness can create clarity. It starts by recognizing the fear-driven pattern, calling it by name, and making a different choice.

In the next section, we'll go deeper into how fear shapes leadership development and why every stage of growth, from early career to executive leadership, brings new fear triggers and new opportunities for learning.

Fear: The Remix

Fear doesn't just show up in organizations. It shows up in us. What we see in meetings—overanalysis, blame, indecision— often reflects the inner patterns leaders are wrestling with inside. The organizational fears we named in the last section are the collective output of individual fear responses playing out at scale. To lead effectively through risk, we have to name both the external dynamics and the internal drivers.

That's where the work of Amon Wolfe comes in. I've referenced Amon several times already because his perspective continues to shape how I think about fear and leadership. As CEO of 432 Hz, Amon's core belief is both simple and powerful. Great leadership happens when mind, body, and purpose are fully aligned. When leaders "tune themselves," they can lead beyond fear. Amon blends performance psychology, adult development theory, stress physiology, and biometric data to help leaders recognize and transcend the ways fear shows up in their decisions and behaviors. His clients include *Fortune* 500 executives, Olympic athletes, military teams, and first responders, people who operate in high-pressure, high-consequence environments.

What drew me to Amon's work was the way science rests on a foundation of humanity. His framework helped me recognize that fear evolves with us. It doesn't vanish as we grow or age; it changes shape. Here's how I've come to interpret fear through stages of leadership development.

At first, fear is about survival: "Will I be safe?" It drives overcontrol, risk avoidance, and nervous system overload. Then it becomes about belonging: "Will I be accepted?" Leaders in this stage tend to conform, overperform, and seek validation. Later, fear becomes tied to identity: "Am I enough?" This often shows up as perfectionism, burnout, or a fixation on outcomes. Eventually, fear becomes more subtle: "Can I grow beyond this?" Leaders begin to make values-based decisions, even when they feel vulnerable. At the highest level, fear transforms entirely: "Am I willing to let go?" This is where purpose leads and action happens without full control. The further we move, the more fear shifts from a threat to a signal. From something we run from to something we move with physically, emotionally, and behaviorally, especially under pressure.

Sidebar: My Own Fear MAP

When I received my own Lead Beyond Fear MAP from 432 Hz, the results were sobering. My fear load was running at 43%, with a stress score of 79 out of 100. Patterns like The Pleaser, The Reactor, and The Righteous One showed up as dominant derailers, each rooted in core fears of exile, abandonment, and meaninglessness. Seeing it quantified made it impossible to ignore. My journey would require me to rework how I carry stress, engage with fear, and lead forward. The awareness wasn't comfortable, yet it was necessary.

Like risk, fear moves in both directions: individually and organizationally, personally and systemically. These developmental stages of fear shape how leaders feel and therefore shape how organizations operate. Until we name and engage with the developmental roots of fear in ourselves, we'll keep creating the same patterns in our teams.

In the next section, we'll look at how fear shows up in group dynamics and how teams can move from fear-based habits to more trust-filled, risk-ready ways of working.

Acting FearFULL

My goal with writing *Trust in Action* was to help leaders move when others hesitate and embrace the urgency required to meet the challenges of our time. I introduced the idea that trust isn't something we wait to feel. Instead, it's something we build through movement. Through our decisions and our leadership presence, trust grows when we show up clearly, consistently, and with the courage to act, even when certainty is out of reach.

So it makes sense that when we turn to fear, the work deepens. This chapter isn't about speed. It's about presence. It's about learning to move forward while fully aware of fear and without letting it control you. If given the chance, it will. Fear doesn't fade with time. It embeds itself into processes, policies, and team dynamics. What starts as a momentary hesitation becomes cultural muscle memory. Leaders start avoiding hard decisions. Teams grow used to overanalysis. Innovation stalls because teams wait for the fear to subside before acting on their terrific ideas.

One of the biggest myths Amon's work helped me debunk is the idea that waiting creates readiness. Delay doesn't dissolve fear. It deepens it. Physiologically, fear builds when left unaddressed. Stress loads increase. Biological signals get louder. The nervous system shifts into chronic overdrive. Moving, even imperfectly, releases that stuck energy and allows both body and mind to recalibrate toward action.

Acting fearFULL means leading with clarity, not certainty. It's the decision to take the next right step, even when the full path isn't visible. It doesn't require bold, sweeping moves. It starts with small signals: asking the question no one wants to raise, making the call you've been delaying, saying out loud what others are whispering privately.

These microactions matter because teams watch more than they listen. When a leader shows they're willing to move, even while afraid, it gives others permission to do the same. Fear spreads. But so does courage. And the fastest way to shift a team out of hesitation is for someone to move first. You don't need to eliminate fear. You need to carry it well.

When leaders acknowledge fear and still move forward, they become guides for others. They walk through the fog and then return, not to boast, but to lead the next person forward. That kind of leadership reflects the maturity required to put risk in action.

This final chapter is not a conclusion. It's a threshold. Because risk, when practiced with trust and moved through with fearFULL leadership, always points toward what's next. And with clarity, we move forward, into tomorrow, and Eastward.

10

Eastward

"For last year's words belong to last year's language.
And next year's words await another voice."

—T.S. Eliot

Where Risk Lives

I t starts with a simple phrase: "Mind the gap." The first time I took the London Underground, I didn't think much of it. I heard the announcement over and over and saw the words painted along the platform edge. It was everywhere, spoken over the loudspeakers, written on the floor, echoing off the tiled walls. And yet, I ignored it. I stood there with my luggage in hand, distracted by everything except what actually mattered, and I missed my train to Paddington Station.

As a first-time visitor to London, I didn't understand the public transit system. The underground map felt like a puzzle, and the signs blurred together. While I stood there overthinking, trying to make sense of it all, the Heathrow Express doors quietly closed. And yes, Paddington Station, like the bear. You'd think with that reference point I would have felt some charm in the moment. I didn't. I just felt stuck, unable to move, trapped between where I was and where I needed to be. That gap, as I've come to understand, is exactly where risk lives.

In London, the trains don't wait for you to figure it out. Conductors announce arrival, passengers disembark and board, and then the train leaves the station. The system keeps moving whether you're ready or not. So I waited, regrouped, and watched for the next train. When it arrived, I stepped on. That day, I realized something simple but lasting: The gap wasn't the enemy, my hesitation was.

Years later, I found myself at another platform, only this time it wasn't physical. It was a call about a life decision. Remember the opening story of this book? Angela, my executive coach, was on the line, and in a tone that was clear, direct, full of care, and just frustrated enough, she said: "For fuck's sake, Massey, don't go back to corporate."

Her voice was my announcement system. Her words were the painted sign along the platform edge. *Mind the gap, Jim.* And I genuinely heard her. Yet hearing and acting aren't the same. I still stepped back. I still stayed on the platform. I wasn't ready. I told myself I was being practical and that going back to a corporate role was responsible, that it made financial sense, and that the timing wasn't right for risk. None of that was the real reason. The truth was, I trusted myself until I didn't.

So why didn't I move forward? Why didn't I take the action that seemed obvious? Because I had another voice in my ear. Someone else who depended on me, someone whose influence shaped my decisions. That voice told me:

"Don't do it. You're so good at working in companies."

"You know how to navigate organizations."

"This is what you do best."

"It's safe. This is where you belong."

At the time, it sounded rational. Supportive, even. Like guidance from someone who had my best interest at heart. But what they were really saying was something else entirely: *Stay small. Stay known. Stay where you won't scare anyone, including me and you.*

Even though I was unhappy and the path didn't feel right, I stayed. Most painfully of all, I stayed despite knowing, deep in my heart, that I was meant for something different. I let fear blind me. The fog of doubt settled in, wrapping itself around the fog of overthinking and the quiet fog of staying small. It blurred my vision of what could be created. Instead of seeing what was possible, I let fear distort my view. I became convinced that playing small was the smarter choice, that shrinking was sensible, and that stepping out on my own was too risky, too reckless, too soon.

Even as I signed the employment contract, I knew none of that was true. And as I sat with that knowing, I began to ask myself: Why? After everything I had built, after all the times I had navigated ambiguity and driven innovation, why had I pulled back now? The answer became clear: I was standing at the edge of the platform, waiting for certainty to arrive, when all I needed was the clarity to step across the gap.

When clarity disappears, fear rushes in to fill the space. Any step I took felt like it could lead to failure. Not just a small failure, but a collapse of everything I thought I had built: my career, my identity, my reputation as someone who knew how to lead change. I feared something that didn't even exist, which meant I stayed stuck oscillating in the Land of Now.

I had proven, time and time again, that I could navigate the unknown. That I could create and deliver in ambiguity. This time, someone else's fear got inside my head. Their scarcity became my ceiling. Their risk aversion became my narrative. As a result, I realized what I lacked wasn't a lack of belief in my own capability; it was a deeper understanding of how to face risk. I didn't yet grasp how trust and fear are always competing for control.

Somewhere along the way, I had been taught to fear risk, which meant I had three options: Manage it, mitigate it, or avoid it altogether. This was the moment I realized risk is simply the space between what is and what could be. It's the space between the platform and the train. The gap.

That's why I've always hated the phrase *change management*. By the time you've planned it, mapped it, and dotted every 'i,' the change has already moved on to what's next. Change doesn't wait for your plan. It happens in real time.

The frustration I felt, sitting there stuck between knowing and acting, came from trying to control something that was never meant to be controlled. So when I finally let go of fearing uncertainty, something shifted. I started exploring the creativity that lives inside not knowing. I started asking myself what I could build. What could I create?

That switch, from fear to trust, from control to creativity is when I stopped standing in the corner while the music was playing. That's when I started dancing with risk. And that brings me back to where this chapter started.

Mind the Gap

That iconic phrase first appeared on the London Underground in 1968. It was a practical and decidedly unpoetic solution. Curved platforms and fast-arriving trains created a small but dangerous gap where people could stumble, get caught, or worse.

Rather than redesign every station or every train, Transport for London installed a simple, repetitive reminder to "Mind the gap." A recording played over and over. The message was painted in bold letters. Why? Because they knew something about human nature. We get distracted. We underestimate the risk. We assume we'll be fine until we're not.

In many ways, that's what life does too. It gives us subtle warnings at first, then louder, then impossible to ignore. For me, Angela was that announcement system. Paddington was the first lesson. My final corporate position was the outcome of staying still, but also the start of something quieter and more powerful.

It marked the slow return of clarity and the chance to build trust in a new direction.

This book is the reminder I needed to write for myself, and I hope it becomes one for you too. Every time we approach a gap, we have a choice. If you choose to stay put, I want to ask you why. Is it because you're avoiding a difficult conversation? Is it a risk you're afraid to take? An opportunity that feels just out of reach? Or a truth about yourself that feels too uncomfortable to face? If so, I hope you'll remember the Face Frame Forward model.

The longer we wait, the wider the gap begins to feel. The more we hesitate, the more intimidating it becomes. What starts as a few inches, something we could easily step over, can, over time, start to feel like a canyon.

At some point, you have to stop staring at the space between where you are and where you want to be. You have to stop asking for certainty and start trusting that clarity comes in motion.

Unknown Caller

When things are uncertain, it's natural to feel afraid. We've been taught to treat the unknown as a threat, to see uncertainty as something to control, avoid, or outsmart. But fear feeds the illusion that staying still is safer than moving forward.

Looking back, it's easy to see how each path, right or wrong, brought us to where we are. Hindsight is not a compass, and we don't get to go back. All we can do is choose to move forward.

The way we've been taught to think about risk is broken. We've been told to fear it, manage it, reduce it until all we've really done is reduce ourselves. We stay trapped in old systems, outdated roles, and self-imposed limits. Ultimately forgetting we are more than what we've become.

We have a choice. Risk doesn't have to get in the way. We can make it the way if we choose to see risk as an invitation. The call to leave the Land of Now and step toward the Land of Next.

When we trust ourselves, and I mean truly trust ourselves, we begin to see the unknown as more familiar than we imagined. We realize we've faced hardship before, we've overcome, and we can do it again.

We face the truth of what's in front of us. We frame what matters with wisdom, clarity, and heart. And then we move forward, not blindly, but boldly. Risk becomes a practice of choosing growth over comfort, courage over control, love over fear. This is a mindset that can cause a transformation. A way of living that lets us release every outdated control someone else placed on us and walk toward the future we're here to create.

Insight to Action

Self-evolution is the backbone of modern leadership. In today's ever-shifting environment, the most critical horizon for growth is internal. The ability to examine biases, challenge outdated behaviors, and rewrite the narratives we've outgrown is what separates stagnant leadership from transformational leadership.

Change on the outside requires change on the inside. When we choose to evolve, to turn the skin inside out and face our own truths, we build the muscle to lead others through the unknown. In this era, self-awareness is essential for navigating complexity.

The world is in constant transformation, and yesterday's strengths aren't enough to solve tomorrow's problems. Traditional horizon scanning associated with risk management can no longer just focus on anticipating external disruptions. Now we must also have the courage to confront our own internal stagnation. Today's leaders must develop capabilities never before required. They need to read market shifts as clearly as they read themselves, examining assumptions, confronting fears, and adapting in real time. Navigating risk demands depth. It requires us to face our own blind spots, own our growth edges, and evolve continuously.

That's what self-leadership looks like in an age of disruption. Like a snake shedding its skin, we release old patterns by necessity. Yet true growth isn't about leaving the skin behind. It's about turning it inside out and wearing it again, exposing new layers of purpose and courage we never knew were there.

Others had always seen me as authentic, the one who gave love freely, without condition. What no one saw was how that love stopped at the surface of me. So I didn't shed to grow. I reversed the very skin I lived in. I took the love I'd always shown to others and let it touch the parts of me I'd kept hidden.

That metamorphosis, that folding inward of everything I gave away, wasn't a change into someone new. It was the first time I truly met the person everyone else knew me to be. This is the risk of becoming. And it's how we prepare for what comes next.

We've been horizon scanning for our entire careers. Looking eastward toward rising threats, emerging regulations, shifting stakeholder expectations. But for too long, we've been stuck reacting to yesterday's risks while tomorrow's opportunities slip past unnoticed.

Most business leaders aren't reading Bloomberg board diversity trends alongside California disclosure laws, UK gender representation data, and Australia's ESG enforcement rollouts. Nor should they be. The risk many leaders face today is information overload without interpretation or the luxury of time.

Risk requires a significant amount of data analysis with context. Headlines become signals, and without expert input, leaders are flying blind. The shift is from reaction to realization. From scanning the horizon for threats to recognizing signals of opportunity. The risks we face now demand anticipatory leadership. The kind of leadership where we close the gap between today's uncertainty and tomorrow's potential.

One company that exemplifies this shift is Belgian insurer Ageas. In 2024, they partnered with an AI firm to scan vast data sources, which included everything from patents to social media, in order to detect weak signals in real time. This collaboration was about framing what mattered and moving before the world told them to.[1,2]

Face: Ageas acknowledged the growing external and internal complexity of global ESG expectations and consumer trust erosion.

1 "Horizon Scanning 2024: Navigating Trends, Strengthening Elevate27," Ageas, February 20, 2025, https://www.ageas.com/en/newsroom/horizon-scanning-2024 -navigating-trends-strengthening-elevate27.

2 "The Trends to Watch in 2024 and Beyond," Ageas, January 26, 2024, https://www .ageas.com/en/newsroom/trends-watch-2024-and-beyond.

Frame: It interpreted this not as a regulatory burden, but as a strategic opportunity to reposition their offerings and build deeper stakeholder alignment.

Forward: The company acted by adapting product portfolios, engaging 2,000+ employees across continents, and aligning investment decisions before new mandates arrived.

This isn't just scanning. It's seeing. It's sensing. It's self-leading in the face of uncertainty. And it's exactly what Eastward means. Choosing to face what's emerging, frame it with clarity, and move with purpose.

Shine Your Light

Leadership is about knowing how to move forward when the path is uncertain and the stakes are real. Looking eastward means leading *into* risk, not around it.

Eastward is both a direction and a product. It's a metaphor for choosing the light, what's emerging, not just what's ending. Horizon scanning becomes more than surveillance. It becomes strategy and staying relevant.

The Eastward platform allows continuous context-setting, real-time alignment, and sense-making for leaders. It brings the right signals into view, frames them with expertise, and guides real-world decisions that align with values and outcomes.

In learning to move through risk, we unlock our own trust. We find our own power, and we learn how to lead our teams, our organizations, and, along the way, ourselves. When you look to tomorrow, when you look Eastward, remember you've got this. Risk isn't what holds you back. It's what sets you free. The future isn't written. It is calling.

Trust leads us to action through Do. Fear moves us through fearFULL when met with clarity. Risk calls us Forward when faced head-on. When we choose to act with clarity, we begin to move toward what's next. So turn Eastward. Face the light and move forward. The next chapter isn't in this book. It's in you. The world is waiting.

About *the* Author

Jim Massey is a trusted advisor to leaders navigating complex risk and transformation challenges. As the founder of Eastward, he helps organizations turn uncertainty into opportunity through innovative risk intelligence platforms.

Jim has held senior executive roles in publicly traded global organizations, where he has consistently helped companies turn bold aspirations into real-world transformation. At AstraZeneca, he built the company's first sustainability program and led its evolution from traditional environmental management to pioneering one of the world's first corporate net-zero commitments. His team's leadership in corporate sustainability helped shape global standards and shifted industry expectations.

Jim has also worked to bring promises into practice. At Zai Lab, he helped bring transparency that drove pay equity and leadership equity across all levels, encouraging other organizations to move from future goals to present mandates. Rather than waiting for the future, Jim helps organizations recognize that the future is already here. Today, he advises leaders on how to make the key decisions that embed the most efficient ways to run global systems, transforming what many aspire to become into what they actually are.

Jim is the author of *Trust in Action* and a frequent speaker on leadership, risk, and organizational change. Today, he collaborates with thought leaders across disciplines to explore human performance at the intersection of fear, trust, and risk in complex systems.

He believes that the greatest risk in leadership today isn't failure; it's relevance. His work focuses on helping leaders and organizations cross the gap between where they are and where they need to be, using risk not as a barrier, but as the way to innovation and growth.